JUBILEE
AND
SOCIAL
JUSTICE

KIM TAN

JUBILEE AND SOCIAL JUSTICE

a dangerous quest to overcome inequalities

Nashville

CONTENTS

CONTENTS

FOREWORD

L. Gregory Jones

Kim Tan's vision and impact are marvels to behold. I remember being captivated the first time I met him and he began describing the work he is doing around the world. The more I learned, the more inspired I became. I discovered how deeply connected his work is with his Christian faith. I learned about the remarkable ways in which he identifies leaders for his projects. Kim described the diverse business models he uses with investors and employees to meet needs and cultivate abundance for everyone involved. And then he showed me the metrics of success he carefully analyzes to be sure that intentions and impact are closely correlated.

His personal story is quite impressive. Born in Malaysia, he moved to England as a teenager and became a Christian. He was drawn to the Anabaptist tradition and the witness of communal life they practice. Vocationally, he became a biochemist, and started a highly successful company in England. After selling the company, he started work as a philanthropist, and then realized that no matter how many checks he wrote, he probably wasn't going to be able to affect the plight of the poor very much. So he became a social entrepreneur, focused on new activities aimed at transforming circumstances for the sake of the common good—especially, in Kim's case, focused on bringing people out of poverty.

The range of his projects is quite extraordinary. A game park in South Africa provides jobs, cares for the land and animals, and provides opportunities for under-resourced kids to participate in the beauty of God's creation. A technology-based education initiative in multiple countries provides amazing results for kids at a tiny fraction of the cost of many other programs. A call center in a prison in Singapore provides job training, wages, and opportunities for prisoners to connect with their families—and has a remarkably low recidivism rate for prisoners once they are released compared to the rest of the country. A project in the Philippines gets women away from sex trafficking and teaches them photo editing skills for real estate companies in the United States. And the list goes on. It seems as if every time I talk with Kim, he has another project underway somewhere in the world.

The business models for these initiatives vary, linked to the needs and hopes of diverse investors. He designs for sustainability and social impact. He assesses leaders of his projects based on their character, with traits such as humility, perseverance, and honesty high on his list as requirements.

These accomplishments are in and of themselves impressive. What impresses me even more, however, is Kim's Christian commitment and the coherence of his vision. This book is an indication of that commitment and coherence. He has studied the Scriptures and the witness of the early church as a framework for his own vocation and his vision for social innovation. And he integrates that study with his practice and organizations in beautiful and impactful ways.

Kim is a contemporary exemplar of Christian commitment to social innovation and impact that has characterized Christians at our best through the centuries. Indeed, my late friend Greg Dees, known as "the father of social entrepreneurship as an academic discipline," having founded programs at Harvard, Stanford, and Duke's business schools, said to me shortly before he died that he thought it was important to reestablish connections between people of faith and social entrepreneurship. Dees noted how often in American history, and the history of the world more generally, people of faith had been at the forefront of innovative initiatives that produced significant social impact across multiple sectors: education, health care, food security, housing, and a variety of businesses. Across the centuries Christians have also been at the forefront of innovation in technology (including farming techniques) as well as wine-making and beer-making. Dees noted to me, though, that he was perplexed by the fact that too many Christians in the United States seem to have lost interest in social entrepreneurship and innovation.

By stark contrast, Christians in the majority world have been doing more social innovation than we often are aware of, and Kim Tan's remarkable vision and impact are at the forefront of such initiatives. He also weaves together Christian thought, knowledge of capital markets, and an imagination focused on empowering people—especially the poor and those on the margins—for new life in the future.

The opportunity to showcase Kim and his work through this book is extremely important. In my book *Christian Social Innovation* (Abingdon, 2016), I call for Christians to rediscover an imagination and commitment to social innovation. But my call was relatively short on examples. I wish I had known Kim when I was working on that book. I am delighted now to have his new book to commend to readers, and to learn more about his important and exciting work around the world.

Kim's vision in this book is a contemporary expression of what my colleague Kavin Rowe calls *Christianity's Surprise* (Abingdon, 2020). Kavin points to the spread of the early Christian movement and how closely it was tied to social innovation and impact. Indeed, the power of that innovation often led others, including the Roman emperor Julian the Apostate, to a sense of envy because of how attractive the Christian witness had become.

The vision of Kim's book calls for radical commitment and transformation for Christians, and for us to take the call to social justice seriously. Yet he gives us a new and re-newed vision for biblical social justice that breaks apart our conventional political categories of conservative or progressive and empowers people for new organizations and new life. This is a radical and dangerous book in all sorts of good and life-giving ways.

In a time when Christians have become too often known for what we are against than what we are for, Kim Tan's vision and impact are especially compelling. When I have shared with young adults examples of what Kim is doing, they often ask how they can learn more. I hope readers, especially young adults, will be inspired by Kim's vision and develop their own commitment to an imagination for Christian social innovation. And then I hope all of us will put these ideas and others into practice, bearing witness to the life-transforming good news of the gospel—for others and for us.

AUTHOR'S WARNING

My friend Malcolm, an investment fund manager, sat opposite me and said, "You shouldn't have written this book. It's dangerous!" He wasn't referring to this book but an earlier work, *The Jubilee Gospel* (2012). He had just re-read it while on holiday. My reply was that he was (1) a glutton for punishment, reading the book twice; (2) he was crazy to read it on holiday (in Spain!); and (3) join the club of those whose lives have been challenged, "messed up," and "inverted and diverted" by the message of the Jubilee.

When I *discovered* the Jubilee, it turned my life upside down. It led me to live in a community where we practiced economic sharing, and challenged me about my addiction to materialism and how I handled wealth. It shaped my investment philosophy and led me to build businesses to alleviate poverty in Africa.

Not many Christians have the appetite like my friend Malcolm to read *The Jubilee Gospel*, which is a biblical exposition of the Jubilee from the Old Testament to the New and throughout church history. It is a "heavy" read. Hence this "lighter" version with less biblical exposition and more on the practical and the modern implications of Jubilee.

Jubilee is a radical and subversive message. Readers have been warned. But if after reading this, you are challenged and your life is turned "upside down," then welcome to the club. I would love to hear how your life has been turned upside down.

INTRODUCTION

Jubilee is a rich idea woven through the storyline of the Bible. Yet we don't hear many Christians talking about it today. More than just a concept, Jubilee is an ancient vision for life that God gave to the people during the early days of Israel's story. Much of the Old Testament is a record of Israel's successes and failures toward living as a Jubilee people. The New Testament continues with Jesus, in his manifesto, proclaiming Jubilee as "the year of the Lord's favor" (Luke 4:19), a central part of his mission.

What is Jubilee? The year of Jubilee that Jesus referred to was meant to take place every fifty years among God's ancient people. Liberty was proclaimed throughout the land as debts were cancelled, land returned to families, and slaves were set free (Lev 25:10, 41). However, this special year was the climax of other legislation that regularly improved the living conditions of former Egyptian slaves migrating to the land of Israel. The "Jubilee principles" infused the teachings of the Israelites on matters such as loans, interest rates, taxation, land ownership, and social structures. Jubilee was a vision of God's humanitarianism, God's justice, and God's vision of a just society.

Jubilee is rooted in God's desire that people live in *shalom*, a rich Hebrew word that we might today describe as complete well-being and wholeness—spiritual, material, relational, emotional.

An important aspect of shalom is the experience of freedom from slavery. The captivity and oppression of the Israelites in Egypt offended and moved God to liberate them (Exod 6:1-8). Slavery is so opposed to God's intentions that God instructed the Israelites to remind themselves of their deliverance from it in the Passover feast every year (Exod 12:14-17). It was to be a memory that would thoroughly shape the way they treated others (Deut 5:15; 15:15; 16:12; 24:18, 22). In a sense, the Jubilee programs were the practical outworking of God's command to "love the LORD your God with all your heart, all your being, and all your strength" (Deut 6:5); and to "love your neighbor as yourself" (Lev 19:18). Love expressed in terms of justice for others leads to shalom (well-being, Isa 58:6-7).

These instructions help us see the shape of God's justice and compassion. Justice shines as one of God's key attributes in the Bible. Isaiah describes the Messiah's mission as one who "established justice in the land" (42:4). In Isaiah 61:1 (the passage Jesus quotes in his Lukan manifesto) the word for "prisoners" or "captives" was not simply referring to the criminal sense but to people who were shackled by economic and social conditions from which there was no escape. Furthermore, "release" here is the same term used in Leviticus 25 to refer to the Jubilee proclamation of liberty. There can be no justice without freedom.

Jesus intends his disciples to follow his manifesto and proclaim Jubilee! Justice is not a side issue (Matt 23:23-34). We are to seek first God's kingdom and divine justice/righteousness (*dikaiosune* is the Greek term in Matthew 6:33 and can be translated as "justice"). That's why understanding the Jubilee really matters, because it's at the heart of the kingdom that Jesus proclaimed.

This book is in two parts. We begin with a survey through the Old Testament on the Jubilee program as given in the covenant to Israel at Mount Sinai. Its idealistic vision, followed by the failure of Israel to practice this instruction, will be outlined. We trace the Jubilee practices in the New Testament through the early church and later church history. The second part focuses on modern expressions of Jubilee as it has caught the imagination of various individuals and groups working out different aspects of the Jubilee in their lives.

PART 1

JUBILEE: A BIBLICAL COVENANT

Chapter 1
JUBILEE AND NATION BUILDING

Undoubtedly the birth of the church on the day of Pentecost was a pivotal event in the story of salvation. Pentecostals have helped us understand Pentecost from the perspective of the gifts of the Spirit, and rightly so, as Peter himself referred to the prophet Joel in explaining the drunken behavior of the early disciples. However, we will see that a better perspective leads to understanding Pentecost as the giving of the Torah at Sinai. Both events are about the formation of a new nation or kingdom. At Sinai, the new nation was imagined as twelve discordant tribes of over two million ex-Egyptian slaves. At Pentecost, a new nation (a royal priesthood) was formed around twelve disciples. At Sinai, it was the giving of the Torah (*torah* means "Teaching" rather "the Law"). At Pentecost it was the giving of the law of the Spirit. The external Teaching summarized in the Ten Commandments (Exod 20) on stone tablets at Sinai is now written on tablets of human hearts (2 Cor 3:3), recalling the new covenant of Jeremiah 31:33 and Ezekiel 36:26. Both events were accompanied by fire and supernatural manifestations and resulted in new distinctive lifestyles. The fire at Sinai is linked to the tongues of fire at Pente-

1

cost.[1] To this day, the Jews celebrate the Feast of Weeks (*shavu'ot*, known in Greek as "Pentecost" and meaning "fifty") as the anniversary of the giving of the Torah, because it took the twelve tribes fifty days of desert wandering before arriving at Sinai.

God's strategy for self-revelation was to call a people and form them into a model nation who would be different from the other nations. This nation would be distinctive in every aspect of their culture and daily lives. So what were the distinctives of this new nation? How should they live with their God and each other?

1. Worship: no more human sacrifices, no sophisticated temples, no sexual orgies, no idols

2. Government: God is the ruler in a theocracy, not a monarchy; commandments are based on justice and mercy.

3. Social relationships: instruction is given for dealing with relationships with parents, members of opposite sex, neighbors, slaves, and foreigners.

4. Diet and disease: definitions of clean and unclean foods, ritual purity (e.g., handwashing), quarantine from disease that causes impurity

5. Economics: even in "mundane" economic life, God wants Israel to be different from the other nations. For a start, each family will be allotted their own land in perpetuity, and the land is to be farmed to provide income. In retrospect, they would all become landowners.

God had promised his people that they will go from being slaves to owners of real estate when they enter the land. This was truly

1. David H. Stern, *Jewish New Testament Commentary* (Clarksville, MD: Jewish New Testament Publications, 1992).

remarkable and is but one indication of the incredible generosity of God as he shapes these former slaves into a confederation of tribes, a new nation that would reflect God's character. They had asset-based capital with which to create wealth and care for their families as well as their communities. This was revolutionary. They recalled a feudal system back in Egypt where all land was owned by kings and noblemen and where they were slaves. From slavery to tribal land ownership—with a monarchy along the way—that's quite a journey. It lays the foundation for ownership of private property, the basis for what we would call a "free market economy" where trade and the exchange of goods and services can take place.

Land was apportioned by lot and according to the size of the tribes (Num 33:53-54). So each extended family was able to build their house and carry out farming in peace, in contrast to their time as immigrants from Egypt. But in divine providence God foresaw that everything would not work out fine for everyone all the time. Some ended up with fertile land, remembered for example, by the psalmist: "The property lines have fallen beautifully for me; yes, I have a lovely home" (Ps 16:6). Others who ended up with poorer land struggled. Furthermore, in an imperfect world, there will be droughts, pests ruining crops, accidents and deaths to key family members, and inevitably, overconsumption. Over time people would fall into debt and would be forced to sell their land and migrate into towns to look for work.

With wisdom from God, the leaders protected the poor from perpetual exploitation. There were teachings on lending: "If you lend money to my people who are poor among you, don't be a creditor and charge them interest" (Exod 22:25; see also Lev 25:35-38; Deut 23:19); requirements for gleaning and harvesting:

"When you harvest your land's produce, you must not harvest all the way to the edge of your field; and don't gather up every remaining bit of your harvest. Also do not pick your vineyard clean or gather up all the grapes that have fallen there. Leave these items for the poor and the immigrant; I am the LORD your God" (Lev 19:9-10; see also Deut 24:19-22). Moreover, all the numerous festivals were occasions when the poor could get meat and cakes from the temple offerings. No wonder these festivals were such significant events and that Jews celebrated them with anticipation and joy.

But the most comprehensive teachings that revealed God's desire for this nation to live as a just society are spelled out in three programs:

THREE-YEAR (TITHING YEAR; DEUT 14:22-29; 26:12)

The tithe (or "tenth part") specified here is of the crops produced from the land. This was to be taken to "the location the LORD your God will select from all your tribes to put his name there, as his residence, and you must go there" (Deut 12:5) and there to be eaten in God's presence. "By returning a tithe to God regularly, the people would learn to fear the Lord (5:23) and know that their prosperity did not depend on irrigation or advanced agricultural techniques, but on the beneficence and provision of their God."[2]

At the end of every three-year cycle, the tithe was not to be taken to the sanctuary to be eaten but to be set aside for certain marginalized groups of people. God required the nation to bring

---

2. Peter C. Craigie, *The Book Of Deuteronomy*, NICOT (Grand Rapids: William Eerdmans, 1976).

one-tenth of their possessions to the town center ("Leave it at your city gates," Deut 14:28) and to invite the widows, orphans, immigrants, and Levites to take what they needed. Imagine churches worldwide doing this even one day a year! I have a dream that someday this will happen globally.

SEVEN-YEAR (SABBATH YEAR OR *SHEMITTAH*; DEUT 15:1FF; LEV 25:1-7)

Every seventh year, God required the nation to do three things: (1) proclaim a one-year holiday for the land, animals, and servants (which means opposition to exploitation of people, animals, and the environment); (2) cancel all debts (because God has canceled our debts for violation of the covenant); and (3) release all slaves (because God has set us free, and Israel didn't enjoy being slaves in Egypt).

Debt happens for a number of reasons: overconsumption, drought, accidents, disease, and poor stewardship of the land. The sabbath year acknowledges the reality of debt but limits its duration so that it is not passed on to successive generations and invariably results in bondage (compare for example the Dalit brickmakers in India).

FIFTY-YEAR (JUBILEE YEAR; LEV 25:8-55)

The Jubilee is the culmination of these programs, which is why it was called the "sabbath of sabbaths." On the fiftieth year, God required the nation to do the three things required during the sabbath year: (1) a year's holiday for the land, animals, and servants; (2) cancel all debts; and (3) release all slaves. In addition, however, God required the land that had been sold during the previous forty-nine years to be returned to their original owners. Now just get your head around that! Good news for the poor. Bad news for the rich who have amassed wealth, unjustly. The Jubilee was a reset button to prevent the kind of situation where the rich get richer and richer and the poor become poorer and poorer. The Jubilee affirmed the following principles:

1. God allows his people to own property so they can provide for themselves and their communities. Capital is needed in order to create wealth. Poverty results from an absence of capital—either asset-based or intellectual capital. Clearly God envisaged some form of ownership that is compatible with free market capitalism *but* with a twist, as we shall see.

Ownership of the land is given to each family and was to be protected and to remain within the family and clan for as long as possible. And you were not to cheat by moving your neighbor's boundary stone to enlarge your own field. So serious was this offense that it was spoken of several times:

> Now in the land the LORD your God is giving you, in your allotted property that you will receive there, you must not tamper with your neighbor's property line, which has been previously established. (Deut 19:14)

> Cursed is anyone who tampers with their neighbor's property lines. (Deut 27:17).

> Don't remove an ancient boundary marker;
> don't invade the fields of orphans,
> for their redeemer is strong.
> He will bring charges against you. (Prov 23:10-11)

6

Naboath's refusal to sell his land to King Ahab (1 Kings 21) is an example of the Jubilee instruction in Leviticus 25:23: "The land must not be permanently sold because the land is mine. You are just immigrants and foreign guests of mine." We are "resident aliens" (Lev 25:47 NRSV). By thinking like ancient Israel, we could imagine all our property as living through a fifty-year leasehold on land belonging to God. Our ownership fits in the broader scope of Jubilee justice.

2. God wants his people to rediscover family. The concept of a nuclear family was unknown during ancient times. Families lived as extended 3G (generation) or even 4G families and would include slaves and other servants. On the Day of Atonement (or Day of Reconciliation), when the ram's horn is blown to signal the beginning of the Jubilee, a mass migration would have happened across the land as people returned to their family homes. The result of this is the reuniting of family members who have been dispersed and been out of touch for years.

3. God wants the people to rediscover shalom. What do families do when they are reunited after a long period of absence? They have meals together, they chat, they laugh and cry together, sharing tales as they "sit underneath their own grapevines, under their own fig trees" (Micah 4:4; Zech 3:10). The Jubilee calls families and communities to embody the community of justice and holiness that the Torah outlines. In this Jubilee shalom, we catch a glimpse of the perfect community of God on earth.

4. The Jubilee was a reset button to prevent poverty and inequalities. It is essentially a fifty-year leasehold system where land is valued according to the number of harvests before the Jubilee year. It is about new beginnings. If one generation failed in their farm, the next generation

7

would have an opportunity to do better after the Jubilee. Conversely, if parents had done well and bought other farms, returning the land at the Jubilee meant that the next generation would also have to work for a living instead of living off their inherited wealth.

To really understand the incredible impact of this program, we need to look at the fifty-year grid below:

1	11	21a+b	31	41	
2	12a	22	32	42a+b	**a** **3-yr**
3a	13	23	33a	43	
4	14b	24a	34	44	
5	15a	25	35b	45a	**b** **7-yr**
6	16	26	36a	46	
7b	17	27a	37	47	
8	18a	28b	38	48a	
9a	19	29	39a	49b	**c** **50-yr**
10	20	30a	40	50c	

In a fifty-year period, the three-year program (labeled *a*) would have been practiced sixteen times, the sabbath-year program (labeled *b*) seven times, and the fiftieth-year program (labeled *c*) once. But notice the triple whammy. Year forty-eight would have been a three-year program, the forty-ninth year a sabbath year, and the fiftieth year the Jubilee year. Intersperse these programs—with the festivals, the weekly shabbat, instructions on lending, gleaning, and harvesting, responsibilities of the extended family, clan, and tribe—and we have a social safety net in part statutory (mandated by Torah teaching) as well as voluntary (families caring for each other).

While some ancient scholars are clear that the forty-ninth and fiftieth years were to be consecutive sabbath years of no work (e.g., the rabbinic interpreter Rashi), more recent evangelicals contended that this would have been impractical.[3] But so is marching around Jericho seven times led by musicians or Gideon's reduced "army" of farmers with pitch forks for weapons. In all these instructions, God is teaching the nation to trust the Lord for their protection and provision. It's a radical way of living in a new economics. It's neither unbridled capitalism nor is it an idealistic communism.

This is *Jubilee capitalism*, where lease possession is given by God to families so that they can provide for themselves, their extended family, clan, tribe, and the poor and marginalized in their community. The extended family unit was the foundation of

---

3. G. J. Wenham, *The Book Of Leviticus*, NICOT (Grand Rapids: William Eerdmans, 1979). Most modern biblical scholars think that Jubilee was idealistic or utopian and not likely implemented. One particular implementation challenge might be timing for those who start "their lease" three or four years before the next scheduled Jubilee year.

the nation, and it was the basis for creating wealth and sharing it with the needy.

We need to remember that all these instructions were retroactively imagined at Sinai before the nation entered the land of promise. To emphasize that these sabbath-year and Jubilee teachings were part of the Sinai covenant, it's repeated, "The LORD said to Moses on Mount Sinai. . . ." (Lev 25:1). According to Rabbi Rashi, "Scripture by mentioning it (*again*) intends to teach regarding every Divine command that was spoken to Moses that in every case they, their general rules and minute details originated at Sinai."[4] Had I been one of the slaves, I would have asked, "What kind of a 'crazy' God have we left Egypt to follow?" The answer would have been a God who loves righteousness and justice and wants to see social holiness as the distinctive identity for this new nation.[5]

> You saw what I did to the Egyptians, and how I lifted you up on eagles' wings and brought you to me. So now, if you faithfully obey me and stay true to my covenant, you will be my most precious possession out of all the peoples, since the whole earth belongs to me. You will be a kingdom of priests for me and a holy nation. (Exod 19:4-6)

God's purpose in leading the twelve tribes out of slavery in Egypt was to form them into a new community—a community of priests, a holy nation distinguished by their Jubilee economics as much as their style of worship and governance. A "kingdom of priests" did not mean that everyone was to be a priest. This was an intercessory role to represent the people before God. Only

---

4. Rabbi A M Silverman, ed., *Chumash with Rashi's Commentary* (Jerusalem: Silbermann Family, 1934), Vayikra, 113.

5. Alan Kreider, *Journey towards Holiness: A Way of Living for God's Nation* (Scottdale, PA: Herald Press, 1987).

one tribe was chosen for liturgical functions in the meeting tent (tabernacle). The rest were involved in building an economy and a functioning society.

Incidentally, Israel was the first tax haven in the world. Because Israel initially didn't have a king (and therefore palaces, servants, clerks) nor a professional army (rather volunteer tribal warriors), there was no need for taxation to run a monarchy or government. Of course, every Israelite was required to pay a temple tax as part of the census (Exod 30:11-16) and required to pay the tithes (e.g., Lev 27:30-33), but no other tax was required. It was only when the nation wanted to be like the other nations and wanted a king who could lead them out to battle that taxation started in Israel. All this despite the warnings by the prophet Samuel:

> "This is how the king will rule over you," Samuel said:

> "He will take your sons, and will use them for his chariots and his cavalry and as runners for his chariot. He will use them as his commanders of troops of one thousand and troops of fifty, or to do his plowing and his harvesting, or to make his weapons or parts for his chariots. He will take your daughters to be perfumers, cooks, or bakers. He will take your best fields, vineyards, and olive groves and give them to his servants. He will give one-tenth of your grain and your vineyards to his officials and servants. He will take your male and female servants, along with the best of your cattle[a] and donkeys, and make them do his work. He will take one-tenth of your flocks, and then you yourselves will become his slaves! When that day comes, you will cry out because of the king you chose for yourselves, but on that day the Lord won't answer you."

> But the people refused to listen to Samuel and said, "No! There must be a king over us so we can be like all the other nations. Our king will judge us and lead us and fight our battles." (1 Sam 8:11-20)

The whole purpose of forming a holy nation was for Israel *not* to be like the other nations, trusting in their military capabilities, but to instead trust in God as their Lord. In wanting to be governed like the other nations, to live like them, Israel rejected the Lord God with terrible consequences. With rare exception, the story of Israel's kings was one of disaster leading to a civil war and captivity for both the northern and southern kingdoms.

Israel came to understand that holiness doesn't only mean putting away idols, faithfully observing the sabbath observance, and regulating the diet with kosher food. It also meant a deeper holiness in every aspect of their lives. In the well-known teaching from Leviticus 19:2 "You must be holy because I, the LORD your God, am holy," the teaching goes on to instruct the nation not to harvest the edges of their fields and vine (19:9-10), not to hold back the wages of a hired man overnight (19:13), not to mistreat immigrants (19:33), and not to use dishonest scales (19:35). This is practical social holiness.

And ultimately this distinctive social holiness is so that God "may be present among them" in relationship (Exod 25:8; 29:45; Lev 26:11; Num 35:34). Israel was chosen to be God's model society, an example for the other nations, and a living advertisement of a holy nation.

God made an incredibly bold promise to the nation that if they obeyed these commandments, "there won't be any poor among you" (Deut 15:4). Alongside this astounding promise was also a threat. If the nation didn't obey these teachings, God would proclaim against them a sabbath, the likes of which they could not imagine (Deut 15). This would be a sabbath not of freedom but of captivity. Since Jubilee was part of the covenant God made with Israel at Sinai, it was a part of the Instruction from Moses.

When these teachings are not obeyed and the covenant broken, there are consequences.

But for a few isolated attempts (Jer 34; Neh 5:1-12), there is no evidence that any of the three Jubilee programs was systematically practiced, and the promise that "there won't be any poor among you" was never fulfilled. Boaz is one of the few examples we have of someone who practiced the instructions for gleaning as well as kinship.

Because the Jubilee programs were never widely practiced, injustices and inequality abounded. Hence the cries of the prophets:

Amos: "But let justice roll down like waters, and righteousness like an ever-flowing stream" (Amos 5:24). "Hear this, you who trample on the needy and destroy the poor of the land . . . in order to buy the needy for silver and the helpless for sandals" (Amos 8:4-6).

Micah: "And what the LORD requires from you: to do justice, embrace faithful love, and walk humbly with your God" (Mic 6:8).

Isaiah: "Remove your ugly deeds from my sight. Put an end to such evil; learn to do good. Seek justice: help the oppressed; defend the orphan; plead for the widow" (Isa 1:16-17). "Doom to those who acquire house after house, who annex field to field until there is no more space left and only you live alone in the land" (Isa 5:8).

Hosea: "The princes of Judah act like raiders who steal the land; I will pour out my anger like water upon them" (Hos 5:10).

Jeremiah tells us that in fact it was because the nation did not observe the sabbath year that they were taken away into captivity by the Babylonians.

Therefore, the LORD proclaims: Since you have defied me by not setting your fellow citizens free, I'm setting you free, declares the LORD, free to die by the sword, disease, and famine! And I will make you an object of horror for all nations on earth. . . . The officials of Judah and Jerusalem . . . I will hand over to their enemies who seek to kill them. . . . I will make Judah a wasteland, without inhabitants" (Jer 34:17-22).

God warned that if the people did not voluntarily give rest to the land and the animals—that is, proclaim a sabbath year—he would do so by forcibly removing the people from the land into exile. Why? Because Jubilee was a key part of the covenant God made at Sinai. Jubilee offered to them true justice and a life of shalom. So the practice of Jubilee was not optional. Neglecting the Jubilee lifestyle led to captivity and injustice. Salutary lesson for us all.

Chapter 2

JUBILEE IN THE
NEW TESTAMENT

Despite the few attempts to practice it, Jubilee largely became a distant vision, a hope carried by the prophets for when Messiah will come and bring in a kingdom of shalom and justice, righteousness and social holiness, when all Israel will be able to enjoy shalom sitting under their vines and fig trees (Mic 4:4; Zech 3:10). Isaiah in particular dreamed about this:

> The LORD God's spirit is upon me,
>   because the LORD has anointed me.
> He has sent me
>   to bring good news to the poor,
>   to bind up the brokenhearted,
>   to proclaim release for captives,
>   and liberation for prisoners,
>   to proclaim the year of the LORD's favor. (Isa 61:1-2)

Five hundred years later these words would be used by the carpenter from Nazareth as the mandate for his ministry (Luke 4:21): "Today, this scripture has been fulfilled just as you heard it," he said to an astonished audience. The favorable year of the Lord mentioned in the Isaiah passage is the ancient Jubilee year. In announcing his ministry with the words from Isaiah 61, Yeshua (Jesus's Hebrew name) was in effect saying that the Jubilee program, which had not come to fulfillment in ancient times, was by no means dead. God is still interested in a people characterized by social holiness, and Yeshua and his disciples are the agents for bringing this into being.

The exact practice of returning land may not have been possible anymore, because the vast majority of the people were landless, being descendants of those who had returned from exile. Nevertheless Jubilee principles are inseparable from the covenant community and need to be expressed in new ways for a new generation. As we have seen earlier, the principles behind returning land during the Jubilee was to enable each family to farm and provide for themselves, to avoid intergenerational indebtedness and inequalities. Jubilee was a reset button to prevent a permanent underclass living in poverty. It was a system designed so that "there will be no poor among you" (Deut 15:4 KJV). God weeps when the poor cry out against injustice and exploitation, but rejoices in communities where there is social justice and social holiness. At last, Yeshua the Christ (Messiah) is bringing in the long-awaited kingdom, and this realm looks like Jubilee revamped. He reinterpreted the Jubilee radically, making it an *everyday event*, a lifestyle rather than one that occurs every fifty years. His reinterpretation gives guidance to how his disciples should express Jubilee for each generation and situation. Some scholars believe that John the Baptist started his ministry in a sabbath year and that Jesus announced his Nazareth mandate in an actual Jubilee year. He reinterpreted it to suit a nation living as taxed subjects of the Roman Empire where the vast majority were poor, dispossessed, and landless. Furthermore, as the prophets foresaw, the

Jubilee mandate would also include spiritual liberation as well as freedom from slavery and "rest for your whole being" as well as physical shabbat.

The ministry of Yeshua and the church have therefore to be viewed from the perspective of Jubilee. For example, Yeshua's practice of the common purse with his disciples (Luke 8) was a new expression of family sharing for everything in common—meals and material possessions. His group of disciples were a microcosm of the new way of living out Jubilee. Most importantly, if the Jubilee mandate was good enough for Yeshua's ministry, shouldn't it be good enough for ours as well? His was a holistic mission—a program of social holiness—unlike some of our modern missions that seek to make only converts, not disciples.

In this microcosm of a holy nation, the Jesus community expressed a radical new lifestyle. They had all things in common, sharing a common purse, and trusted God to provide for their needs. Social holiness was evident among them, and the poor and social outcasts seem to be attracted to them. They had a higher standard of behavior, living "beyond" the law. They had the sense of an extended family at peace with themselves and with each other. Shalom and shabbat rest were experienced, and their mission was to share this good news with everyone as they traveled around Israel or later into the Roman Empire. Moreover, Jesus had redefined what it meant to be "family," which is one aspect of Jubilee: "Whoever does God's will is my brother, sister, and mother" (Mark 3:35; Matt 12:50). And to his mother, "Woman, here is your son," and to the disciple, "Here is your mother" (John 19:26-27). Christians were to be a family in the broad and concrete sense of the Jubilee. Families share all things and care for each other. Families feel a sense of obligation to those in their midst and fulfill those responsibilities out of love.

The common purse practiced by Yeshua and his little community for three years is the context to understand some of the most difficult sayings of Jesus about wealth.

> **Luke**: "Don't be afraid, little flock, because your Father delights in giving you the kingdom. Sell your possessions and give to those in need. Make for yourselves wallets that don't wear out—a treasure in heaven that never runs out. . . . Where your treasure is, there your heart will be too" (Luke 12:32-34).

> "Good Teacher, what must I do to obtain eternal life?" Jesus replied, . . . "Sell everything you own and distribute the money to the poor. Then you will have treasure in heaven. And come, follow me" (Luke 18:18-19, 22).

I have never heard a sermon on these difficult sayings. In commentaries and on the very odd occasion when they have been discussed, there has always been some caveat such as, "It is only for the rich young ruler who had a problem with his wealth and materialism" (and we don't, really?) or that "it applies only to a select group of really spiritual types who want a monastic life." I think these instructions regarding spiritual treasure can only be understood in the context of the Jesus community. He's inviting them to sell their possessions and join his community, where they share a common purse. Not sell your possessions and live on love and fresh air! Although Jesus called his disciples to a challenging renunciation of personal property, he did not ask them to live without material goods and needs. The disciples still possessed money—money in common used to further their mission and help those in need.

The Jews believed that when Messiah came, he would usher in a new era of justice and wholesome shalom, where justice would roll down like rivers, sickness should be no more, and the lion would lie down with the lamb. Jesus's cry for justice and mercy echoes the prophets Amos, Micah, and Isaiah.

> **Matthew**: "How terrible it will be for you legal experts and Pharisees! Hypocrites! You give to God a tenth of mint, dill, and cumin, but you forget about the more important matters of the Law: justice, peace, and faith" (Matt 23:23).

> "[The Human One] will separate [the nations] from each other, just as a shepherd separates the sheep from the goats. . . . 'Inherit the kingdom that was prepared for you before the world began. I was hungry and you gave me food to eat. I was thirsty and you gave me a drink. I was a stranger and you welcomed me. I was naked and you gave me clothes to wear. I was sick and you took care of me. I was in prison and you visited me'" (Matt 25:32, 34-36).

Jesus's practice of giving to the poor draws on the three-year program of Jubilee, but transformed into a daily habit and community structure (John 13:29). Instead of giving to the poor every three years as instructed in the Instruction from Moses, this generosity and sense of mercy was to characterize the lifestyle of this community.

For instance, Jesus's teachings in the Beatitudes (or "beautiful attitudes") takes up the Jubilee themes: "Happy are" the poor, those who are hungry now, those who weep, the shalom makers (Matt 5; Luke 6). His instructions to "lend expecting nothing in return" (Luke 6:35) is drawn directly from the sabbath year instruction to cancel debt. To lend without expecting to get anything back is another way of saying "cancel the debt."

The Jubilee is also at the heart of the Lord's Prayer (Matt 6:9-13). The word *forgive* is the Greek *aphesis*, which means to "release or cancel." ("Debt" is *opheilema* and "trespass" is *paraptōma*). We can translate the debt clause in the Lord's Prayer as "Cancel our debts [*opheilema*] as we also cancel the debts of our debtors . . . because if you release others when they trespass [*paraptōma*] against you, your heavenly Father will also release you."

Without being instructed, Zacchaeus responds to Jesus with echoes of Jubilee generosity and mercy. "Look, Lord, I give half of my possessions to the poor. And if I have cheated anyone, I repay them four times as much" (Luke 19:8). Zacchaeus, having experienced extraordinary mercy and grace, responds with an act of generosity that surprised everyone, even Jesus. Zacchaeus goes beyond what the law required with this act of generosity.

By words and deeds such as these Jesus was radically reinterpreting the Jubilee, making it an everyday duty in the lives of his disciples rather than an event that takes place every fifty years. And this condition of perpetual Jubilee had a new name: the "kingdom of heaven" (in Matthew's Gospel or "kingdom of God" in Luke's Gospel). This was Yeshua's main message: "Change your hearts and lives! Here comes the kingdom of heaven!" (Matt 4:17). Many of his parables start with phrases grounded in immediate economic experience: the kingdom of heaven is like a mustard seed, a king who settles dispute' yeast, treasure hidden in a field, merchant looking for fine pearls, landowner in a vineyard (Matt 13). This kingdom wasn't some distant place or time; it was the immanent, ongoing rule of God in the lives of Jesus followers, expressed in the fruit of Jubilee actions and attitudes. It is a fulfillment of Exodus 19:6: "You will be a kingdom of priests for me and a holy nation."

What we see in the Gospels is only the beginning of a fresh attempt by Jesus and his disciples to work out Jubilee kingdom principles in a new era of economics and politics. The full expression of this will only become evident in the Acts of the Apostles, to which we next turn.

The pervasive health-and-wealth doctrine that emerged as a twentieth-century heresy is the half-truth that God has promised prosperity to those who have faith and who glorify him by their luxurious lifestyle. After all, why should the son of the King live like a pauper, they say? If this were true, Jesus wouldn't have said, "Sell your possessions and give to those in need. Make for yourselves wallets that don't wear out" (Luke 12:33), or "Sell everything you own and distribute the money to the poor. . . . And come, follow me" (Luke 18:22), or "The Human One has no place to lay his head" (Luke 9:58). And Zacchaeus would not have given half his possession away to the poor.

In *Desiring God: Meditations of a Christian Hedonist*, John Piper describes such Christians:

"By an almost irresistible law of consumer culture (baptized by a doctrine of health, wealth and prosperity) they have bought bigger (and more) houses, newer (and more cars), fancier (and more clothes), better (and more) meat, and all manner of trinkets and gadgets and containers and devices and equipment to make life more fun."[1]

---

1. John Piper, *Desiring God: Meditations of a Christian Hedonist*, rev. ed. (Colorado Springs, CO: Multnomah Books, 2011).

The tragedy is that this kind of teaching is prevalent in low income countries among the poor, who are exhorted (and pressured even) to give so that they may receive God's blessings of health and wealth. Typically the only beneficiaries of this kind of teaching are the pastors who live a life of luxury while the congregation continues in their poverty. This kind of spiritual extortion is of the worst kind because it is done in the name of one who was born in someone else's house, a refugee, worked with his hands as a carpenter/builder and shared all he had with his band of followers. This is the modern-day equivalent of the medieval practice of selling indulgences in return for spiritual blessings or escape from purgatory.

Malachi: "Bring the whole tenth-part to the storage house so there might be food in my house." Malachi 3:10 is a reference to the three-year tithe, not our modern-day understanding of tithing. As such, the yearly tithe was to be consumed by the community, including the Levite priests. It wasn't meant exclusively for the Levites. Once every three years, a tenth of all income was meant for the poor. See chapter 4 for more on this practice during early church history.

Chapter 3
JUBILEE AND PENTECOST

Pentecost—with its supernatural manifestations of a mighty rushing wind, tongues of fire, and people speaking in tongues or languages—triggered the questions that led to Peter's proclamation of the gospel. These men were not drunk. They had been filled with the Spirit. This was what Joel had prophesied would happen. Most evangelicals would endorse the centrality of Peter's proclamation, while charismatic Christians might emphasize the supernatural signs that accompanied the proclamation. However, for me, the greatest miracle at Pentecost was not the supernatural manifestations. It was the sight of new believers selling their assets, sharing their goods and daily meals with strangers who had become their newfound family members, and creating a new community that, astonishingly, cut across all existing racial, economic, and social lines.

This economic sharing was truly miraculous. Remember, these after all were Jews on pilgrimage to Jerusalem for the Passover! This takes us back to the Jubilee and Sinai. This was the birth of a new nation, the new people of God formed around the Twelve disciples. God was giving the Spirit this time to write spiritual instructions on tablets of human heart, not on tablets of stone.

The coming of the Spirit led to a spontaneous new expression of Jubilee. Granted, the Twelve disciples had had some experience of this community for three years with Yeshua. Even so, there was a spontaneity (led by the Spirit) as they coped with this explosive growth in new family members, many of whom were poor. This emerging community lived out Jubilee in a fresh way for a new generation in a very urban setting. This new, supernaturally generous community had a "wow" factor that attracted thousands to join them.

The early church grasped the comprehensive nature of the gospel as their new faith affected every aspect of their lives, including their pockets. Theirs was a whole-life discipleship, not the dualistic faith of many modern Christians. They manifested the radical transformation of the gospel in the very structures and activities of their community.

Jubilee in the Hebrew scriptures was a radical socioeconomic program that would have resulted in social holiness for the Israelite nation. It was an imaginative, humanitarian program involving a year's holiday to discourage exploitation of the land, animals, and slaves. There was also a requirement to forgive debts, release slaves, and return all properties bought in the forty-nine years to their original owners. Along with wealth creation, there was a blueprint for wealth distribution in order to create and maintain a just society.

We observe that all the Jubilee principles were also evident in this new community of Christ followers:

1. Despite attempts to describe the economics of the early church as communism, it is better described as a form of compassionate Jubilee capitalism. Believers apparently still owned private property, which was implied as a lease in the

original Jubilee provisions. They opened up their private houses each day to share meals. The story of Barnabas, in contrast with the story of Annaias and Sapphira, showed that properties belonged to most new believers, and that their giving was voluntary rather than coerced.

2. The church at Pentecost rediscovered a new meaning for family. All those born of the Spirit, calling God their Father, belonged to the same family, irrespective of race, social status, or gender. As Kavin Rowe demonstrates in *Christianity's Surprise*, chapter 3, Christianity introduced the surprising new notion of all of humanity as united in Christ, the new Adam.[1] The gospel's identification of each person with Christ, especially the lowly, prompted Christians to construct new creative structures, which fit this new understanding. In other words, the revelation of Christ gave a new pattern for how to understand social holiness. As new brothers and sisters, they cared for one another spiritually, emotionally, materially, and economically. They embarked on a huge program of feeding thousands of widows, orphans, and strangers every day.

3. They rediscovered shalom. There was forgiveness and healing—physical, emotional, spiritual. There were restored relationships. Their material needs were being met. "Great grace was upon them all" (Acts 4:33). We see a new community formed of restored people, sharing their lives, welcoming strangers with confidence into their midst, feeding the widows, and generally at peace having favor with God and humanity. Unlike notions of a dualistic gospel, Christ's gospel brought both spiritual and material restoration.

---

1. C. Kavin Rowe, *Christianity's Surprise: A Sure and Certain Hope* (Nashville: Abingdon, 2020).

The last question the disciples asked Jesus before his ascension was, "Lord, are you at this time going to restore the kingdom to Israel?" After three years of following Jesus, they had still failed to fully understand the nature of the kingdom that Jesus was ushering in. The expectation of the Jews was that when Messiah came, he would deliver Israel from Roman occupation and become king over a united Jewish nation, as it was recalled under Saul, David, and Solomon. They were expecting self-rule to be restored to Israel. Jesus's answer is instructive: "It isn't for you to know the times or seasons that the Father has set by his own authority. Rather, you will receive power when the Holy Spirit has come upon you, and you will be my witnesses in Jerusalem, in all Judea and Samaria, and to the end of the earth" (Acts 1:7-8). In other words, Jesus is telling the disciples that they don't have to worry about when self-rule will be restored to Israel. But what they will see is the formation of a new messianic kingdom when the Holy Spirit comes upon them in a new way of living as the people of God. They will see a holy nation, a Jubilee kingdom ushered in by the Holy Spirit.

As we observed in the previous chapter, Jubilee as imagined in the Old Testament probably wasn't implemented throughout Israelite culture. It's not clear that it was ever carried out by the nation of Israel. Why? Probably because it was too costly and radical. It couldn't be carried out with mere human effort because of our selfishness and addiction to materialism. Such is the transformative power of the Spirit to break down racial and economic barriers, to set us free from our greed and selfishness, and to give us a new heart that empowers us to live as citizens of a new kingdom. The Jubilee promise, "won't be any poor persons among you" (Deut 15:4), was finally fulfilled at Pentecost through the power of the Spirit: "and there were no needy persons among them" (Acts 4:34). Only through the coming of the Spirit was it possible to love one another in this radical way. The true sign of being full of the Spirit is extravagant generosity. Likewise a Spirit-filled church will overflow with expressions of generosity toward its "family" and community and beyond.

Karl Marx was inspired by the attractiveness of the Acts community. But his vision for communism didn't rely on the transformative power of the Spirit to enable community members with different social status to care for one another. He glossed over the human need for private ownership of properties and that sharing this wealth is done voluntarily. The Acts community wasn't a prototype of communism. It was a new society, whose social justice allowed for private ownership within the larger context of responsibility and care for the poor, and for volunteerism. It was a result of the newfound love they had for one another (including immigrants and total strangers) because of the outpouring of the Spirit. It was also a result of the new revelation of what it was to be human in light of Christ. They saw the unity of humanity in the image of God and established new structures that would enable them to live the new gospel ethic. Like Marx, I too was inspired by the radical lifestyle of the Acts Community. It is what caused me to think more deeply about becoming a follower of Jesus. But where we differ is over sharing wealth through state coercion and enforcement rather than a voluntary church community that is sharing resources in response to the demands of the gospel and the love of the Spirit. The Jesus community with their common purse was the first time it could be said that "there were no needy persons among them."

If Yeshua used the Jubilee mandate as his mission, should we not follow the Master? If so, how do we express Jubilee through the church for our generation that longs to be "wowed" by something real and radical? How do we build communities that can manifest and embody a true and lasting social holiness?

Bishop Lesslie Newbiggin captures this well:

> When Jesus left the earth, he did not leave behind a book, or creed. . . . He left behind a visible community that the world might see [and we add: and see what kind of a kingdom and ultimately what kind of King he is.] The church invisible needs to become visible. Like her Lord, she needs to become "flesh and dwelt among us" so that the world may behold His glory.[2]

---

2. Bishop Lesslie Newbiggin, *The Household of God* (Eugene, OR: Wipf and Stock), 1953.

Chapter 4

JUBILEE IN
EARLY CHURCH HISTORY

As the early Christian community grew larger and more structured, Christians reflected more concretely on how to live the radical new social holiness of the gospel. A letter was sent by Mathetes to a man by the name of Diognetus; thought to date from the second century, it described the early Christians in this way:

> They live in their own native lands, but as aliens; as citizens, they share all things with others; but like aliens, suffer all things. Every foreign country is to them as their native country, and every native land as a foreign country. They marry and have children just like everyone else; but they don't kill unwanted babies. They offer a shared table, but not a shared bed. They are at present "in the flesh" but they don't live "according to the flesh." They are passing their days on earth, but are citizens of heaven. They obey the appointed laws, and go beyond the laws in their own lives. They love everyone, but are persecuted by all. They are unknown and condemned; they are put to death and gain life. They are poor and yet make many rich. They are short of everything and yet have plenty of all things.[1]

---

1. From a multichapter letter by Mathetes to Diognetus, circa 130 to 200 CE. The original letter is lost; only one copy existed in a thirteenth-century manuscript that was lost in an 1870 monastery fire.

This was a radical lifestyle, one that made the Christians stand out from the crowd. The Spirit's presence in their lives was evident, enabling them to go "beyond" the requirements of law in their attitude and behavior. They were citizens of another kingdom, and yet that didn't stop them from immersing themselves in the needs of the world around them. Following in the footsteps of Jesus, theirs was a wonderfully incarnational faith.

Their approach to material goods was rooted in the principles of simplicity, solidarity, and generosity. "They offer a shared table, but not a shared bed." In the development of the early church, the surprising, new notion of human solidarity in Christ continued to shape church structures and activities. Tertullian, writing during the same second-century period, expressed it similarly: "We who are united in mind and soul have no hesitation about sharing property. All things are common among us except our women."[2] The boundaries they established between themselves and their neighbors were necessitated by purity, not greed.

COMMUNITY OF GOODS

Here, then, were Christians set free by the Spirit to share and give radically in order to support the poorer members of the body, the orphans, the widows, the prisoners, and even non-Christians. They describe tithing as insufficient, surpassed by Christ's even more radical call to generosity. It had been a requirement of the Old Covenant and had been fulfilled in Christ and extended in his teachings to his disciples. The coming of the Spirit had kin-

---

2. Tertullian, *Apology* 39.11.

dled *koinonia*, a far more "glorious"[3] dynamic, because it sprung from the bonds of love rather than the constraints of law:

> And instead of the tithes which the law commanded, the Lord said to divide everything we have with the poor. And he said to love not only our neighbours but also our enemies, and to be givers and sharers not only with the good but also to be liberal givers towards those who take away our possessions. . . .

> Now all these, as I have already observed, were not [teachings] of one doing away with the law but of one fulfilling, extending, and widening it among us; just as if one should say, that the more extensive operation of freedom implies that a more complete subjection and affection towards our Liberator had been implanted within us.[4]

Those who came to church would bring money as well as food (oil, cheese, olives, bread, wine) as their offering. The poor brought water for diluting the communion wine. By the third century, clothes and shoes were also mentioned as contributions. These offerings would be placed on a table by the entrance and distributed by the deacons to the needy, including any absent from the meeting for various reasons.

How extensive the community of goods was practiced is not clear. But there is considerable evidence that church communities expected their members to give supplies extensively to support those in need. Certainly by the third century, giving to the church for the sake of the poor had become central to Christian practice.[5] In Northern Africa, Cyprian (bishop of

---

3. Cf 2 Cor 3:7-11.
4. Irenaeus, circa 200, *Against Heresies* 4.13.3.
5. Peter Brown, *Poverty and Leadership in the Later Roman Empire* (Hanover, NH: University Press of New England, 2002), 42.

Carthage 248–258) exhorted the rich to see giving to the church as the best means of supporting those in need. As an effective steward of these communal resources, Cyprian was responsible for directing the alms to those with needs of various kinds. In short, the sharing of material goods was universally taught and practiced by the early church.

Here are a few examples:

> All things are common, and the rich are not to be avaricious. . . . And it is not right for one to live in luxury, while many are in want. How much more glorious is it to do good to many than to live sumptuously! How much wiser to spend money on human beings than on jewels.[6]

> Let the strong take care of the weak; let the weak respect the strong. Let the rich man minister to the poor man; let the poor man give thanks to God that he gave him one through whom his needs might be satisfied.[7]

> These contributions [that is, put into the church's treasury] are the trust funds of piety. They are not spent on banquets, drinking parties or dining clubs; but for feeding and burying the poor, for boys and girls destitute of property and parents; and further for old people confined to the house, and victims of shipwreck; and any who are in mines, who are exiles to an island, or who are in prison merely on account of God's church—these become the wards of their confession. So great a work of love burns a brand upon us in regard to some. "See," they say, "how they love one another."[8]

---

6. Clement of Alexandria, circa 200, *Instruction* 2.13.20.6.
7. Clement of Rome, circa 100, 38:2.
8. Tertullian, circa 200, *Apology* 39.5-11.

LOVE FEASTS

Another important way in which mutual love and care was expressed in the early church was by means of the love feast (or agape meal, as it is also called).

The love feast was an integral part of the church's corporate life. Celebrated daily in apostolic times, and then weekly in later years, it consisted of a communal meal to which all were invited. Unlike the majority of modern-day services, the pattern of service in the early church consisted of a love feast followed by prayers, preaching, and then Holy Communion. Just as the disciples and Jesus had shared the Passover meal before they shared the bread and wine, so the early church enjoyed an agape meal together before sharing Communion.

The love feast served two important functions. Not only did it build up the body in an act of mutual sharing and fellowship, but crucially it also ensured that the poorer members were able to enjoy a nutritious meal at least once a week. Each person brought along whatever food he or she had in order to share it with the others. No matter how little some of the poorer members contributed, they were free to help themselves to what the richer members provided. Portions were also sent to the sick and housebound.

This was Paul's vision of economic koinonia—the rich person voluntarily supplying the poor person's needs so that equality might ensue. The practice recalled the sharing of manna among the Israelites in the desert (see Exod 16:15-18), and thanks to the enabling of the Spirit, it grew out of the shared bonds of Christian love and teaching. The radical new view of Christ in every believer led Christians to envision a bond between rich and poor in their Christian community—a bond Roman society had never previously imagined.

Here is William Barclay's description of the feast:

> To that feast everyone brought something, just as he was able. They pooled everything that was brought and then they sat down to share it out together. At this feast all kinds of people were sitting together. Many of the early Christians were very poor; some of them were slaves. A slave's rations in Greece were a quart of meal a day with a few figs and olives and a little wine vinegar. Very often this common meal on the Lord's Day was the only decent meal the slave got all week, and he only got it because in that early Church everyone shared with everyone else everything he had. If the spirit of Christ is really in us we will not be able to be happy if we see someone else in need and don't help him.[9]

Although we can't know all the details of this practice or how widely it was practiced, meals and worship became central places for early Christians to provide for one another. These meals enacted the Jubilee justice of God in practices that brought shalom to all in the new family of the church.

> Our feast explains itself by its name. The Greeks call it agape, i.e. affection. Whatever it costs, our outlay in the name of piety is gain, since with the good things of the feast we benefit the needy.[10]

The love feast as an integral part of the church's service was short-lived. In the period following Paul's death, worship gradually became more formal, focused around set prayers, and love feasts were detached from the rest of the Sunday service. Holy Communion became the focal point of the church's corporate life. Love feasts continued to be celebrated for a time, but in the

---

9.　William Barclay, *God's Young Church* (Philadelphia: Westminster Press, 1970).

10.　Tertullian, *Apology* 39.16.

evening, as a separate activity from the morning service. However, local churches continued to sponsor and organize food provision for poor community members. For instance, many early churches in northern Africa had large storehouses adjacent to their worship facilities. Eventually the same abuses that Paul had contested in 1 Corinthians 11:20-22 (drunkenness, greed, disorder) probably led to the disappearance of the love feasts as a distinctive of the church's life.

By the end of the third century, the church had traveled a long way from its early, informal origins. But as Kavin Rowe notes, structure and hierarchy emerged almost immediately so that the church could provide for its vulnerable members (see Acts 6). As he argues, a well-functioning structure is seen in its ability to creatively solve problems without "becoming fully enmeshed in the details of that solution."[11] Just as deacons seemed to adequately address the early issue of providing for orphans, early Christians in the second and third centuries also used the developed structures of the church in order to live the Jubilee lifestyle.

By the third century, the church had also become more institutionalized. This was inevitable to cope with the growing numbers and needs of the church. Structures and programs were formalized and gradually became institutions. A distinction was appearing between the role of the clergy and the laity. Churches were given property and money by their members for the support of the needy in their midst. This money was given sacrificially "to God" and also "for the poor," and bishops and other appointed clergy became the natural overseers of these resources.

---

11. C. Kavin Rowe, *Christianity's Surprise: A Sure and Certain Hope* (Nashville: Abingdon, 2020).

Although early Christians would sometimes talk about this giving as a "tithe," we should not think of this as a percentage tithe. Instead, the wealthy heard a constant refrain of preaching exhorting them to radical generosity, depending on their means. Clergy called them to give based on the Jubilee principle of the gospel: since the poor are part of the new family of Christ, those who are able should give all they can to bring shalom to others. By giving to the church to provide for the poor, the wealthy helped to enact the justice of God in social holiness. Sometimes these gifts could be significant. But the bulk of Christian care for the poor in the first few centuries derived from the consistent gifts of those of moderate means. We need to remember that the majority of the Christians in the first few centuries were slaves with little means. By living a Jubilee lifestyle, church communities were able to pool together a considerable amount of money and other goods to help the needy. But in the fourth century, the scale and possibilities of social holiness began to shift even further.

So for three hundred years, despite discrimination and persecution, people took the risky step of being baptized and entering into the life of an exciting but despised religious minority. The Jubilee lifestyle of koinonia sharing and sacrificial giving was a key part in attracting people to become Christians. For the most part, the church relied on Spirit-inspired leadership to develop life-giving institutions that cared for the poor in a time of rapid growth and expansion. And then the emergence of Emperor Constantine I in the early fourth century changed the church.

CONSTANTINE'S CONVERSION

Perhaps the most surprising aspect of early Christianity is its success. Christianity emerged as a marginal part of Judaism in Roman Palestine and four centuries later became the faith of emperors. Although Christianity was not illegal in the Roman Empire, Christians in the first few centuries experienced sporadic persecution in parts of the Roman Empire. Many lost their lives. One of the most famous stories from the period is that of Polycarp, the bishop of Smyrna (69–155 CE). After refusing to offer incense on an altar to Caesar, and refusing to call the emporer "God," he was tied to a stake and burned. His executioners urged him one last time to save his life by confessing Caesar's divinity, but Polycarp replied, "Eighty and six years have I served Him, and He has done me no wrong. How then can I blaspheme my King and Saviour?"

Such noble acts of martyrdom were not uncommon during the first three centuries of Christianity. But the most severe empire-wide persecution from 303 to 305 was to be the last. Significant changes began when Constantine, emperor of Rome (306–337), issued the Edict of Toleration protecting Christians from harm, and also began supporting them. Moreover, Constantine eventually became a Christian himself. With imperial toleration and support of the emperor Christians were in a very different position. The church could grow at a much faster rate with official sanction. From Constantine to Theodosius I's enforcement of Christianity, the number of Christians grew from 5 percent to 50 percent of the imperial populace.[12] It could also now gain the support of

---

12. Ramsay MacMullen, *Christianizing the Roman Empire* (New Haven, CT: Yale University Press, 1984)

many more wealthy Romans than in previous centuries. Thus, Christians entered a new period in which to creatively live the Jubilee in a new context.

Its newfound wealth, power, and respectability would have a profound effect on the witness of the church after Constantine, especially in its attitude toward wealth and the poor. Inevitably, as the church became part of the establishment with its grand buildings and ceremonies, it would lose its emphasis on caring for the poor. This process was, however, gradual, because throughout this period, there were priests and bishops who preached tirelessly about the Jubilee message of justice and shalom for the poor. They continued to expand the gospel's new vision of the unity of rich and poor in Christ and the responsibility to care for each other. More concretely, then, they had created institutions such as storehouses or local monetary funds to care for the poor in their midst.

We take for granted the presence of modern institutions of care. Charities abound. Hospitals are easily accessible in urban areas, even if they come with questions of insurance and payment. But this was not always the case,[13] nor did it have to be so. Until Christianity, the Roman world knew no institutions of this sort. Most care for the needy came—if at all—through family or via networks of patronage and hierarchical dependence. Christianity brought new institutions to the world that strove to embody the radical unity of rich and poor in the gospel in their communities. They created new and innovative institutions that would allow them to recognize the image of Christ in others and bring shalom to them. By doing so, they lived the social holiness of Jubilee.

---

13.   See C. Kavin Rowe, *Christianity's Surprise: A Sure and Certain Hope* (Nashville: Abingdon, 2020).

In the first few centuries discussed above, Christianity was still growing, and churches largely cared for the poor and needy in their own communities. But with the greater prominence of Christianity in the fourth century, Christians could expand their Jubilee lifestyle to include care for poor and needy in the wider community. To take one example, by the 350s Christians had established networks of "hospitality centers" (*xenodocheia*, also called "poor houses" [*ptōchodocheia*]). These institutions took in travelers—sometimes pilgrims, but more often refugees or needy people searching for food and work. With the added benefits of tax relief after Constantine, local churches were able to create and fund more of these to bring wider and more sustainable relief to their communities.

Basil of Caesarea (329–379), also known as Basil the Great, a bishop in Asia Minor, sponsored an influential instance of these "hospitality centers" with a soup kitchen and other community services in Caesarea. But he also created a network of clergy in rural towns of Asia Minor tasked with caring for the needy. In addition to his tireless preaching for the rich to see the poor as part of their own Jubilee community, he also found creative new ways to enact social holiness in concrete practices and institutions. He used the privileges afforded to clergy by Constantine and his successors just as it was intended—for the poor.

Contemporaries describe him as closely involved in the center and its storehouses of food and clothing, even famously greeting lepers with the kiss of peace.[14] It is for actions such as these that bishops were known in the early church as "lovers of the poor." Here is one of my favorite quotes from Basil:

---

14. Brown, *Poverty and Leadership*, 40.

When someone steals another's clothes, we call them a thief. Should we not give the same name to one who could clothe the naked and does not? The bread in your cupboard belongs to the hungry; the coat unused in your closet belongs to the one who needs it; the shoes rotting in your closet belong to the one who has no shoes; the money which you hoard up belongs to the poor.[15]

Of course, the prominence and size of the church also brought new challenges. Structure and organization can lead to deeper and more sustainable forms of social holiness. But it also meant that each individual Christian may not have always felt the total commitment of the gospel. Moreover, clergy began to encounter tension with wealthy Romans who were uncomfortable with their inheritances gifted to the church for the sake of the poor. Many wealthy Christians preferred to build a fancy church with their name on it rather than let their money be used to help those in the community with material needs. Other clergy preached in ways that softened the call for the wealthy to follow the radical call of Jubilee.

Distortions arose as the church and the rulers became more intertwined. The pope was granted new political authority, and Constantine conferred upon himself considerable theological authority. Government money was used to build elaborate church buildings and to subsidize the clergy. Rich landowners built churches for those living on their estates and started appointing clergy to manage them. Those who had not been baptized were obliged by imperial law to undergo a course of instruction on the importance of this rite. Those who still refused to get baptized were severely punished. In such a coercive environment, nominalism inevitably flourished. "Church" came to mean the building

15.   Brown, *Poverty and Leadership.*

rather than the body. People attended rather than belonged. Total commitment was no longer necessary to be a Christian. For many, it was simply a question of expediency.

Moreover, large networks of care require greater maintenance. The question of maintenance and inequality became more pressing. How were all of these church buildings going to be maintained? What about the land that the church now owned, and what about the clergy? How should larger urban churches relate to their poorer rural sister churches?

> By the end of the fifth century the church at Rome had devised a system by which all income from rents and offerings was divided into four parts—for bishop, clergy, the poor, and for repair and lighting of the churches. Elsewhere the distribution varied. Under this system the bishop received an income much greater than that of the priests and deacons—though he had to spend a considerable amount on hospitality. Another contrast was that between rich and poor churches. The wealth of the Roman bishop was enough to make the great pagan senator Praetextatus say, "Make me a bishop of Rome and I will become a Christian tomorrow." The regular income of some country clergy was so small, on the other hand, that they had to rely primarily on the generosity of the Christians of their congregation.[16]

With the emergence of newer structures on a larger scale, churches and other institutions often run the danger of overlooking principles of economic koinonia of the early church. Furthermore, many of the new converts had great riches, but they were not being challenged to share them. The radical approach to wealth of the pre-Constantinian churches was being slowly usurped by something far less demanding.

---

16. Johnathan Hill, *The History of Christianity* (Oxford, UK: Lion Hudson, 2007).

In *Beyond Tithing*, Stuart Murray sums up some of the softer approaches to wealth that were emerging:

> Theologians raided the Old Testament and various secular philosophies to develop a new system that would be acceptable in a much broader church. Among the main components of this system were:

- It was no longer a person's actual wealth that mattered but their attitude toward it: wealth could be retained provided one did not feel bound by it;

- Giving was no longer motivated primarily by concern for the poor but by a concern about one's own soul; the spiritual rewards available to givers were emphasized over the material needs of recipients;

- Giving to others was presented as a good investment: what had previously meant living more simply was now seen as likely to result in God increasing one's wealth;

- The concept of koinonia was replaced by the concept of "almsgiving" and care for the poor was now regarded as an expression of "charity" rather than justice. It became disconnected from the concept of koinonia so that the giver did not see a connection between themselves and the poor they supported;

- Money for the poor was split by the need to maintain church buildings, and providing appropriate financial support for church leaders took precedence;

- Some church leaders began to advocate fixed tithes and abuses emerged.[17]

---

17. Stuart Murray, *Beyond Tithing* (Eugene, OR: Wipf and Stock, 2011).

Although institutions of care were built on the Jubilee responsibility and social holiness of regular contributions to the church, certain kind of fixed tithes also emerged. Churches had long understood that giving to the church was a duty—albeit a duty based on love. But a model of tithing developed that downplayed the radical justice and call to renunciation of wealth that Jubilee involved. It was a return to the law without its broader context. The New Testament witness—what happened at Pentecost, Paul's vision of economic sharing—was gradually minimized. When Christian preachers speak about Christian giving, they tend more often to refer back to the Old Testament model of tithing than to the New Testament model of koinonia.

The tragedy and danger of this approach is not only that it overlooks the witness of the Spirit but also that it represents a diminished version even of the law! Tithing never stood alone in the Old Testament. It came as part of a package that included Jubilee. Koinonia, while surpassing both tithing and Jubilee, embraced the principles of both. When Spirit-led koinonia was and is abandoned in favor of Old Testament models of giving, the Jubilee element of economic justice is grievously overlooked. Why is this so important? Because there is a crucial difference between tithing and Jubilee. Once again, we turn to Stuart Murray:

> Tithing, as a percentage measure, applied equally to everyone, but Jubilee would have markedly different implications for those who were rich and those who were poor. The tithe was concerned with income, whereas Jubilee dealt with capital. By comparison with the social upheaval envisaged by the Jubilee provisions, the tithe involved a fairly minor redistribution of resources in favour of the Levites and the poor. Tithing, unlike the Jubilee, could not prevent the development of a widening gap between rich and poor.[18]

18. Murray, *Beyond Tithing*.

43

By itself, tithing does little to solve economic injustice. It has a mitigating effect, at best. But it serves to salve the conscience of the giver and shields one from any real examination of their attitude toward wealth and neighbor. Moreover, it patronizes the recipient by making the individual a charitable cause and not seeing the poor as one's brother or sister in Christ—someone in the new family of the church.

If people are to be free to enjoy stewardship of God's creation, they need justice, not charity. In the same way that mercy is better than sacrifice (Hos 6:6; Matt 12:7), so justice is better than disconnected charity. One springs from love, the other springs from duty and self-interest.

Although the practice of charity to care for the poor was formalized, the practice of being family, of economic sharing, was lost from the fourth century onward as the church took on the new prosperity and wealth befitting the official religion of the empire. From meeting in homes and catacombs, the Christians now had splendid buildings for their worship. The church was allowed to own land and enormous estates, which were either donated or bought. This change in the economic status of the church was a cause of some embarrassment. The pope even declared that Christ and the apostles were not poor, and it became heretical to teach the poverty of Christ. The established churches have remained powerful economic institutions ever since. With wealth came the establishment of new institutions and a gradual loss of the radical distinctiveness of the early church. This is best illustrated by the story, probably apocryphal, of the pope showing Thomas Aquinas the splendor of the Vatican, saying, "The church can no longer say, 'Silver and gold have I none'" (Acts 3:6), to which

Aquinas replied, "Neither can it say, 'In the name of Jesus Christ of Nazareth, rise up and walk!'"

By the end of the fourth century, the church had undergone a massive transformation compared with its birth at Pentecost. It had seen its numbers grow, its geographical boundaries extended, its status officially sanctioned by the authorities in power, and its influence increased. But at what cost? Its growth brought new challenges. Could it maintain a radical, distinctive approach to economic justice? Would it still act as "salt" and "light" in the world?

Chapter 5
JUBILEE IN RADICAL CHURCH HISTORY

The rapid growth of the church brought new difficulties for its vision of social holiness from the end of the fourth century onward. In the post-Constantinian church, how would Christians maintain a radical, distinctive approach to economic justice?

This question would trouble many over the ensuing years of church history. In this chapter, we are going to spotlight some of the movements and individuals that emerged over the course of church history to challenge the church afresh in its Jubilee witness. Doubtless many others could have been included; the following list is not comprehensive.

MONASTIC MOVEMENTS

Although many today probably envision monasteries as large institutions, the heart of the monastic movement was and is simplicity and renunciation. The earliest monks ("solitary ones" from Greek *monachos*) went to the Egyptian desert to follow the radical call of Christ. One of the earliest and most well-known monks, St. Antony, went to the desert to obey Christ's radical words in the gospel. According to stories told about him, Anthony was a wealthy young man who began to reflect on the radical Jubilee koinonia of Acts 2. One day in church, he heard the reading of Matthew 19:21: "If you want to be complete, go, sell what you own, and give the money to the poor. Then you will have treasure in heaven. And come follow me." When he heard this, Anthony immediately went and did just as Jesus commanded and began living a life of simplicity and renunciation.

Whether or not Anthony was the first monk, many Christians began to take this same approach and attempt to live a simple life of prayer, renunciation of ownership, and giving to the poor. In the early fourth century, an Egyptian known as Pachomius organized a large community of ascetics who would practice Jubilee koinonia together. Those entering Pachomius's communities surrendered their personal wealth to a common fund and were given a simple set of personal items. The monks lived a simple, balanced life, without luxuries but also without extreme deprivations. They had regular meals, regular devotions, and regular work periods. The communities were largely self-supported through such activities as basket weaving, gardening, and other crafts. Some of the money they earned was also given to the poor and others in need.

Pachomius established a pattern of communal monastic life that many subsequent religious orders would use as the basis of their way of life. During the first twelve hundred years of church history, these orders were tremendously important as a reaction and a counterbalance to times of excess in the church. Monks offered a radical image of the gospel's call to renunciation of wealth and service to the poor. Monasteries were some of the first hospitals and had a large role in running the "poor houses" and other care institutions of early and medieval Christianity.

Nevertheless, as with the broader church, just as these institutions enabled a broader, sustainable social holiness, they also introduced new possibilities for abuse. Many of the orders had accumulated vast amounts of land and property. The monks were therefore spending increasing amounts of time managing their estates. The prophetic role of the monastic movement had begun to wane by the early twelfth century. As a result, various monastic reformers in the early and medieval church emerged to bring monastic communities back to the gospel vision of Jubilee koinonia. It seems almost inevitable that movements become established institutions as they grew and expanded over time. These establishments then sparked new protest movements, which over time also became established institutions, and the cycle began all over again.

THE FRANCISCANS

One such fresh witness came in the thirteenth century in the figure of St. Francis of Assisi, an Italian originally known as Francesco di Pietro. He emerged onto the scene in a time when monasticism had become more implicated with ownership and wealth. The Franciscan order appeared, providing perhaps the best example of the monastic tradition's ability to challenge the church to greater social holiness.

Ironically, though, it was never Francis's ambition to found a religious order. His desire was merely to live out a radical understanding of Christian brotherhood, and to challenge others to do the same. With such an attractive faith as Francis's, however, it was not long before his band of brothers had become so large that it became necessary to protect the unity and purity of the community by adopting a rule. As we saw in early Christianity, structures like this emerge in order to enable a more sustainable Jubilee social holiness.

Francis's approach to wealth and possessions was uncompromising. Whereas other orders owned property from which they derived a substantial income, Francis was adamant that his brotherhood would pursue a different path. His brothers would be free, unhampered by material possessions:

> The brothers shall not acquire anything as their own, neither a house nor a place nor anything at all. Instead, as pilgrims and strangers in this world who serve the Lord in poverty and humility, let them go begging for alms with full trust. Nor should they feel ashamed since the Lord made Himself poor for us in this world. That is the summit of highest poverty which has established you, my most beloved brothers, as heirs and kings of the kingdom of heaven; it has made you poor in the things of this world but exalted you in virtue. Let this be your portion, which leads into the land of the living. Dedicating yourselves totally to this, my most beloved brothers, don't wish to have anything else for ever under heaven for the sake of our Lord Jesus Christ.

> And wherever the brothers may be together or meet other brothers, let them give witness that they are members of one family. And let each one confidently make known his need to the others, for, if a mother has such care and love for her son born according to the flesh, should not someone love and care for his brother according to the Spirit even more diligently? And if any of them becomes sick, the other brothers should serve him as they would wish to be served themselves.[1]

---

1.   St. Francis, Rule 6 from *The Rule of the Friars Minor*, 1223.

Francis understood the corrosive effect that riches could have on the human soul, and he wanted his brothers to be free from their power. In his original Rule during 1210–1221, Francis warned that "the devil will blind the eyes of those who desire and appreciate money more than stones. Let us take care, we who have left everything, lest for so small a thing we lose the kingdom of heaven."[2] Material goods were not in themselves bad, but one had to avoid becoming unduly attached to them. Having very little in the first place helped to limit any such attachment. But one also had to willingly surrender the little one had in the face of another's greater need. As one person writes,

> Francis maintained that for a brother not to part with whatever he had to someone poorer was tantamount to stealing from him or her—a harsh ruling for the friars who had virtually nothing to give except whatever food they had collected and their cloaks.

> Cloaks feature in a number of anecdotes—to the despair of the brothers who found it difficult to keep warm clothes on Francis's back during hard weather.[3]

Notice how Francis understood ownership as a matter not of individual giving but of justice. The excess that one possessed was rightfully the property of the poor. But the goal wasn't simply relinquishment of property—though this became an important part of the order. Instead, outward poverty was a manifestation of the spiritual state of the human before God, a form of radical identification with Christ: "although he was rich, he became

---

2. St. Francis, Rule 8 from *The Rule of the Friars Minor*, 1210–1221.

3. Adrian House, *Francis of Assisi: A Revolutionary Life* (Mahwah, NJ: Paulist Press, 2003).

poor" (2 Cor 8:9). Outward poverty manifests one's utmost dependence on God.

But Francis's approach to poverty wasn't primarily built on a negative—the sinfulness of greed, the fear of losing one's soul. It was more fundamentally centered on a positive—the beauty of simplicity, the joy of dependence on God. Because Francis's heart and mind were unfettered by material worries, he was free to enjoy the gift of God's creation to the full. By clearing his heart of attachment to possessions, Francis could love God and others with the fire of intense spiritual love.

For example, Francis had a rare synergy with creation. All God's created beings were Francis's brothers and sisters, and he referred to them as such. The sun, for example, was "brother sun," and the water was "sister water."[4] While we might consider Francis's language amusingly eccentric or redolent of New Age spirituality, it was actually rooted in a sound theology of the stewardship of creation and the created order. It was wonderfully consistent with Jubilee values. Freeing our hearts from materialism allows us to love God and neighbor all the more. We can better live the reality of the new family of God.

We must not make the mistake, then, of reducing Francis to some kind of harmless nature lover. He was far more dangerous than that. The life he lived and the words he preached were deeply challenging to the prevailing culture of the period, both within society as a whole and within the church. They are also deeply challenging to our modern-day culture. In our current era of profit-driven industries and economies, debt slavery and in-

---

4. "The Canticle of the Sun" is St Francis's most famous composition in praise of creation.

tensive farming, we would do well to reflect on the message of St. Francis and imitate his example.

Sadly, the Franciscan Order, as so many other religious orders before it, saw its original fervor and influence decline in the years following its founder's death. Following years of internal conflict, and under pressure from the papacy, the Franciscans eventually became property owners. It was a significant development, particularly striking for the way that it exposed the wealth of the papacy.

> In general the Franciscans accepted that poverty was an ideal practiced by Christ and the apostles. From this arose the idea that the Church hierarchy should remain aloof from entanglements in the world. If extended to the papacy, this put in question the position of the pope as ruler of the princes of Christendom. In addition, the massive wealth of the church as a whole came under scrutiny.[5]

THE WALDENSIANS

A figure contemporaneous with Francis, and just as radical, was a man by the name of Peter Waldo (or Valdes), a merchant from Lyons in France (1140–1218). Much less is known about Waldo or the early Waldensians than about Francis or the early Franciscans, but the little that is known reveals some striking similarities.

Like Francis, Waldo's conversion led him to exchange a life of wealth and privilege for one of poverty and simplicity. Like Francis, he was appalled by the excesses of the contemporary pope and other senior members of the Roman Catholic Church, and

---

5. Tim Dowley and Pat Alexander, eds. *The History of Christianity (A Lion Handbook)* (Colorado Springs, CO: Chariot Victor Pub, 1990).

sought to present an alternative based on the example of Jesus. Like the Franciscans, the Waldensians lived an itinerant lifestyle: "They have no fixed habitations. They go about two by two, barefoot, clad in woollen garments, owning nothing, holding all things in common, like the apostles, naked, following a naked Christ."[6]

This lifestyle embarrassed and riled the papacy. It threw the profligacy of the medieval church into sharp relief. What's more, Waldo made it his aim to translate the Gospels from Latin to French, making the word of God more accessible to the masses. With this work complete, Waldo and his followers enabled more people to encounter the radical gospel call to perfection. Much like St. Antony, Waldo seems to have taken up a life of poverty and chastity in imitation of Matthew 19:21. They argued that their lifestyle represented a more genuinely apostolic form of life than that of the pope and his consorts at the time.

When ordered by the archbishop of Lyons to stop preaching, the Waldensians continued regardless. Eventually their refusal to recognize the authority of the church led to their excommunication. Waldensians were subsequently persecuted by French authorities; many were burned at the stake. But such pressure failed to eliminate them, and their numbers increased. The movement spread and became large enough, such that the French King Francis I sought to suppress it by force. Thousands were massacred and imprisoned with brutal violence by French troops.

Although the orthodoxy of some Waldensian beliefs may have been controversial, their passion for truth and simplicity had prophetic power, exposing the hypocrisy and complacency of the

---

6. Walter Map, *De Nugis Curialium* (Oxford, UK; Clarendon Press, 1983).

established church. They would capture the hearts and minds of those who longed for something more simple and a Jubilee social holiness that was pruned back to essentials. Early reformers in the Calvinist tradition were inspired by their lifestyle and claimed them as early examples of their ideals.

JUBILEE AND REFORMATION

With the rise of many different reform movements in the sixteenth century, the church encountered new ways of living Jubilee in its time. By the late middle ages, the number of mendicants—those living in voluntary poverty, like the Franciscans—had greatly increased. Church and secular officials began to worry about how to discern the true needs of their community and how to allocate resources. The Jubilee witness of monastic poverty needed a renewed face.

To confront this problem, Christians in various major cities began to register the poor and create programs to identify the true needs of the poor in their city. Living in a time where the government handles poverty in a bureaucratic, often impersonal way, it would be easy to see public institutions of care for the poor as inevitable and disconnected from a Jubilee vision. But in Reformation Europe, these programs of cataloging the poor in cities were an innovative and creative means of providing Jubilee justice and social holiness. By attempting to distinguish the various kinds of poverty and locate individuals in need, Christians could better bring about social justice. Many historians see in these early modern poor lists the origins of contemporary charities and social institutions.

But the Reformers went further than developing new ways of caring for the poor. They also returned to the "surprise" of the Christian story. They criticized how the clergy had begun personally to profit from the institutions that were developed to embody the radical call of the gospel to renunciation and care for the poor. The Reformers criticized the "poverty" and "celibacy" of priests and called clergy to once again use the resources of the church primarily to care for those in need.

THE ANABAPTISTS

One of the most radical groups of this kind were the Anabaptists. The term *Anabaptist* denotes a variety of groups that emerged in Europe (originally Switzerland and Germany) in the sixteenth century with a vision for renewing the church. Although in many ways quite diverse, these groups were united in their rejection of infant baptism, believing that a person's baptism should be accompanied by their confession of faith. It was this belief that led others to call them Anabaptists, or "Rebaptizers," as a term of abuse.

But baptism wasn't, in actual fact, the Anabaptists' primary concern. What troubled them most was how the church had strayed such a long way from its origins of simplicity and care for the poor. It wasn't functioning as a connected body united in Christ, but as a complex hierarchical institution where divisions became more and more visible. Most of all, it had compromised its integrity by its accumulation of great wealth originally intended for the care of the poor. With such abuses in view, the

Anabaptists longed to restore to the church its original simplicity and fervor.

To do so they insisted on a radical lifestyle of mutual love and service. They were committed to economic justice and wealth redistribution and saw this as one of their distinguishing characteristics. As one Anabaptist writes,

> Is it not sad and intolerable hypocrisy that these poor people [the Lutherans] boast of having the Word of God, of being the true, Christian church, never remembering that they have entirely lost their sign of true Christianity? For although many of them have plenty of everything, go about in silk and velvet, gold and silver, and in all manner of pomp and splendour; ornament their houses with all manner of costly furniture; have their coffers filled, and live in luxury and splendour, yet they suffer many of their own poor, afflicted members (notwithstanding their fellow believers have received one baptism and partaken of the same bread with them) to ask for alms; and poor, hungry, suffering, old, lame, blind, and sick people to beg their bread at their doors.[7]

The Anabaptists were widely regarded as subversive and rebellious. One of their core beliefs, that Christianity's ethic of nonviolence meant that Christians could not serve in government positions, threatened to rock the very foundations of society. Anabaptists developed their own networks of solidarity and care, but they were seen as a danger. Anabaptists were persecuted by both Roman Catholics and also Protestants, and were even denounced by leaders of the Reformation such as Luther and Zwingli. The Reformers were particularly disturbed that Anabaptists seemed to qualify the principle of justification by faith by emphasizing the importance of works of righteousness. Many thousands were ex-

---

7. Menno Simons, "Reply to False Accusations" (1552).

ecuted, and the majority of those that survived lived a peripatetic existence, constantly on the move to avoid capture.

Like the monks of earlier times, their radical return to principles of Jubilee social holiness make the Anabaptists a powerful prophetic voice to the church. They offer a vision of how to structure communities to embody Jubilee social holiness.

Some of the Anabaptists found refuge in Moravia, where they were able to settle without threat of persecution. By drawing their inspiration from the early church, in 1529 they formed a community called the Bruderhof based on the principle of economic koinonia.

Jacob Wiedemann, one of the original leaders of the Bruderhof, was autocratic, and the movement would not have survived but for the efforts of Jacob Hutter (d. 1536). It is a credit to his leadership that these Anabaptists chose to be named after him even though he was not their founder.

Under the able leadership of men such as Peter Walpot (1518–78) and Peter Riedemann (1506–66), the Hutterites founded some hundred Bruderhofs with a total membership of thirty to seventy thousand. Each Bruderhof was a self-sufficient community where the community of goods was practiced. Men and women were assigned to work according to their abilities. Children were cared for in the Bruderhofs' own nurseries and schools. The Hutterites are said to have enjoyed 100 percent literacy, a remarkable achievement for that time and place.

The Hutterites's lifestyle provided a living testimony of the biblical principle that the pooling of resources works to everyone's advantage. It is not something that the wealthier members should fear, as if only the poor will benefit. Thanks to their communal approach to wealth, goods, and talents, Hutterite brethren prospered economically as well as educationally. It is a pattern of success that endures to this day. They found concrete ways of living a Jubilee community of social holiness where each person could find the shalom of Christ.

As we have seen, Christians have found creative and powerful ways to live Jubilee social holiness across the centuries. In some cases, this meant using the structures of the church to care effectively for the poor in the community. In others, this meant creating smaller communities to offer the broader Church a witness to apostolic simplicity. In our time in which many Christians possess wealth and prestige similar to that of past times, the example of previous Christians living the radical call of Jubilee can inspire us also towards creative social holiness. In part 2, I look at some modern examples of Jubilee practices. Like our historical survey, I pray that these examples can inspire us to develop practices, communities, and institutions which can manifest the Jubilee shalom of the gospel.

PART 2

MODERN EXPRESSIONS OF JUBILEE

INTRODUCTION TO PART 2

We traced expressions of Jubilee from Sinai through the early church into church history. Twelve tribes set free from slavery in Egypt in dramatic fashion expecting to arrive in the promised land within weeks unexpectedly find themselves wandering in the desert for forty years. Moses led them to make a crucial pit stop at Sinai, where the twelve tribes were told that they were to be formed into a new holy nation. For what was later to become Israel the nation, they entered into a covenant with God that they would obey Torah regarding how they should live with one another so that God might dwell among them and be their Lord. Central to what it meant to be a holy nation, to be set apart from other cultures, were the Jubilee teachings. Loving God went hand in hand with loving your neighbor by showing generosity and giving shalom not only to your extended family but also the orphaned, widows, servants, slaves, and immigrants. Even the land and the animals during the sabbath and Jubilee years were to enjoy their sabbath rest. This covenant was on the whole seldom kept, and instead of the social holiness—which should have been a distinctive feature of the new nation—greed, exploitation, corruption, and inequalities came to characterize the people of Israel. The consequences of breaking the covenant were dire, with Jerusalem destroyed and the nation taken into captivitiy in Babylon as slaves. This vision of a holy nation where "justice roll[s] down like waters, and righteousness like a ever-flowing stream" (Amos 5:42) was kept alive by the prophets as they waited for Messiah to usher in the kingdom.

Jesus announced his ministry by proclaiming that he had come to usher in the year of the Lord's favor, the Jubilee year, the kingdom of God. This was his central message. Jesus took what was essentially a dormant program in the old covenant to make it a reality, to fulfill the scriptures about the favorable year of the Lord. It was about good news for the poor, healing the sick, feeding the hungry, giving rest and comfort to all who asked, and creating a new family through sharing a common purse out of love for one another. These were fresh expressions of a kingdom of righteousness, a holy nation.

His timid disciples, emboldened by the coming of the Holy Spirit at Pentecost, proclaimed that Jesus was indeed Lord and Messiah. Just seven weeks earlier, Peter had denied Jesus three times. Now through the power of the Holy Spirit, he preached his first sermon to the temple crowd that this Jesus whom they crucified had been made both Lord and Messiah. And as a result of the outpouring of the Holy Spirit, they saw a spontaneous expression of the messianic kingdom through the daily sharing of meals, selling of properties, and having all things in common. This was truly miraculous. The poor, the widows, and the strangers were fed and cared for on a huge scale so that it was noticeable that "there were no needy persons among them." Here was social holiness exemplified. A visible messianic community. We can now *see* what this Jubilee kingdom looked like. No wonder "the Lord added to their number daily those who were being saved" (Act 2:47 NIV). Those who joined this new community were of one heart and mind and loved and treated each other as family members with God as their Father. The Holy Spirit made possible that which humanly speaking was difficult to practice because of human selfishness.

The church fathers continued this radical and countercultural way of living for some four hundred years. The gospel of the kingdom required a change in belief as well as behavior, and this was done through a program of catechism sometimes lasting three years. With leaders like Clement of Rome, Justin Martyr, Cyprian, Basil, and Tertullian, church members continued to love, care, and provide for each other. Such was the appeal of their kingdom message that it was estimated that some 5–10 percent of the population had become Christian. What was said of Paul's time in Thessalonica was also true for the early church fathers: "These people who have been disturbing the peace throughout the empire have also come here. . . . Every one of them does what is contrary to Caesar's decrees by naming someone else as king: Jesus" (Acts 17:6-7). Christians had a new allegiance to King Jesus and his kingdom of social holiness. Such was their way of living that they often described themselves as "colonies of heaven." Their allegiance to a new King often got them into trouble with Caesar, triggering periodic harrassment.

When the church became part of the establishment through Constantine's conversion, it became harder to maintain the social holiness of Jubilee. Where the church had spread throughout the empires in the first four centuries, the next thousand years saw the church conquered by the world. Nevertheless, radical groups such as the Franciscan, Waldensians, and Anabaptists continued to practice some form of economic sharing and care for the poor. While the mainstream chuches, both Catholic and Protestant, became more and more a part of the establishment, these radical groups sought to return to the primitive roots of their faith, often harrassed for their radical and simple lifestyles that echo Jubilee themes.

Each generation has expressed aspects of Jubilee within the context of their culture and economic environment. What about us? In a society where most of us are not landowners or farmers or business owners, but rather employees and urban dwellers with mortgages and credit card debts—how can we live out Jubilee? Can we even express these Jubilee principles in our personal and church life today? While the practical implementation of Jubilee in Old Testament stipulations (such as returning land or releasing slaves) is no longer the basis of democratic societies, the principles are still relevant to bringing in the kingdom of God. As our brief survey of church history observed, the radical gospel message led Christians in every age to live out these Jubilee principles anew.

We will next look at some expressions or aspects of the Jubilee in our present generation. These features range from economic sharing and having all things in common, to setting the captives free, cancellation of debt, distribution of wealth, feeding the poor, and stewardship of the land.

1. COMMUNITY LIVING
Denzil Road Family

My personal experience of community living took place while I was a student at Surrey University in the UK during the 1970s and 1980s. Our group had no formal name but became known as the Denzil Road family. At its peak, there were about forty of us living in twelve houses, most of which we owned. In line with our understanding of private ownership and Jubilee, we assisted each other in buying our own houses. We gifted each other with sums of money for the deposit, with the balance financed through a mortgage. We did not have a trust or a centralized holding entity for these properties; they were all privately owned, in contrast to other earlier communities. Furthermore, instead of withdrawing to some remote countryside, we lived out our communal life in the town, just as the Acts community did. This intentional community lasted for eight years. For us community was not an end in itself. We saw it as an environment where discipleship could take place. It was an environment for God to deal with our material addiction. We shared our material wealth (the little we had) with our extended family and friends. Surplus financial resources were released to help others. To paraphrase Tertullian, "We had all things in common except our wives *and our books*" (because Christians are not very good at returning borrowed books!), and we could also say, "There were no needy persons among us."

During our time in community, we converted a garden shed that acted as a storehouse. We had a centralized shopping system, buying in bulk to cut costs. Apart from using it for our own needs, food from the storehouse was also used to share with needy students. Would it not be wonderful if churches located near poor communities have a storehouse of food, clothes, household goods where the poor can come and take what they need?

Living in a community was both rewarding and challenging. The friendships we formed were deep and fulfilling and have lasted. We shared countless communal meals together while talking about our faith and "putting the world to rights." Our experience in community stimulated our own personal growth and shaped our worldview. Our challenges included the sacrificial giving of our time and money, lack of private space, and sharing rooms with three, sometimes five others, while writing a PhD dissertation. There was a daily challenge of "feeding the multitudes" made all the more challenging because we never knew how many additional guests would be invited for dinner. And because we believed everyone should be involved in hospitality regardless of their culinary skills, we ate some very "interesting" meals!

But through it all, we learned to love one another and accept each other's idiosyncrasies, which we brought from different countries and backgrounds (my dad called us a mini–United Nations). The community DNA was hardwired into our lives and has endured over the years, even as we moved into the married and family life phase. Some of us have continued living as extended families, with single young adults sharing our homes, epitomizing the ethos of a warm and open house that defined our community. Our community not only reflected different modes of ownership and generosity but also helped us to live out social holiness. We were living out the "new family" of the church and bringing shalom to those around us.

Bugbrooke Community

Bugbrooke started in the UK during the 1970s and was one of the most dynamic and radical communities I saw, until its closure in 2018 due to financial and harassment scandals. It had a centralized ownership of property and owned hundreds of acres of farmland where food was produced. The community undertook amazing work among the marginalized and disadvantaged, who were brought to the community to live and work on the farms as part of their rehabilitation from mental illness, criminal activities, and substance abuse. One can safely say, "There were no needy persons among them." For over forty years, this was a community where they had all things in common and where many broken lives were restored. However, with a centralized trust structure of property ownership, instead of the Jubilee principle of family and kinsmen ownership, it became very difficult for members who wished to leave to take their share of trust assets. Many were hurt and disadvantaged when they tried to leave. This centralized structure also lent itself to authoritarian abuse. The community had a very charismatic leader. The verbal abuse and alleged sexual harassments cannot be condoned; such abusers should be prosecuted and jailed.

Bruderhof Community

This amazing movement, which started in the 1500s, is still in existence today. This is how they describe themselves on their website (www.bruderhof.com):

> We are an intentional Christian community of more than 2,900 people living in twenty-three settlements on four continents. We are a fellowship of families and singles, practicing radical discipleship in the spirit of the first church in Jerusalem. We gladly renounce property and share everything in common. Our vocation is a life of service to God, each other, and you.
>
> We try to love our neighbour and share everything, so that peace and justice become a reality.

The communities engage in a number of businesses to support themselves. Again, their website states their values.

> We commit to:
>
> • Solidarity: Respect for the dignity of all people.
>
> • Ethical practice: We act with honesty and regard the rights and needs of others.

- Workmanship: High quality is an expression of the love we put into our work.

- Stewardship: God entrusted nature to our care and we strive to use and care for it wisely.

The following are some of the businesses they are known for:

- **Community Playthings**, based in New York, Pennsylvania, and the UK, designs and manufactures high-quality wooden classroom and play environments for schools and daycare centers.

- **Rifton Equipment** designs and manufactures adaptive equipment for children and adults with disabilities, allowing children with severe cerebral palsy.

- **Danthonia Designs**, based in Australia, supplies custom dimensional signage.

These are profitable multimillion dollar businesses that provide for all the needs of the community members. As they have all things in common, clearly, "there are no poor among them." They practice the Jubilee justice of the Acts community, and they live out the radical "surprise" of the gospel in solidarity with Christ. They have found concrete and sustainable ways to live social holiness in our time.

Amish Communities

In a similar vein, and just as old as the Bruderhof movement, are the Amish communities. This group split away from the Swiss Mennonites during the 1690s and settled in the United States in the nineteenth century.

The Amish live in small rural communities where strong family and social ties allow them their own distinctive and separate way of life. The family is the heart of Amish community, individual

70

identity and spiritual life. The Amish are well known for their farming. However, in recent times they've diversified from farming and in some communities more than 80% work in small businesses making things like indoor and garden furniture, small sheds, quilts and leather goods.

The Amish produce many of their needs, rearing animals to produce meat, growing corn for food and for feeding animals, and growing vegetable both for food and for sale. Amish women make most of the clothes. But they are not totally self-sufficient and rely on the outside community for other requirements.[1]

In their own way, the Amish communities continue to practice the Jubilee koinonia of the early church through their economic sharing, simplicity of family life, and caring and providing for each other. They too can say "there are no needy persons among us."

Monastic Movements

As we outlined in part 1, the monastic movements had the principle of the common life. All those entering the monastery had to surrender their personal wealth to a common fund. The monks lived simple lives without luxuries, driven by asceticism. They were self-supporting through various activities such as farming and brewing. In addition to supporting themselves, the money they earned was given to the poor and others in need. They established hospitals, schools, and other institutions to care for those in need.

However, although they started out poor by begging for alms, over the years, many of the orders accumulated vast amounts of

---

1.   BBC Documentary 2009-06-23; https://www.bbc.co.uk/religion/religions/christianity/subdivisions/amish_1.shtml.

land and property from donations and trade. Sometimes this enabled monks to pursue sustainable, impactful Jubilee social holiness in their communities. But in other cases the monks had to spend increasing amounts of time managing their estates or were caught up in gaining worldly prestige.

Some criticize this movement because, while they had all things in common, their isolation and withdrawal from the world, their pursuit of asceticism, and a centralized common fund were not features of the Acts community. Any time there is a centralization of money and influence, there will be a greater opportunity for authoritarianism and abuse. It's human nature. As the old edict states, power corrupts; absolute power corrupts absolutely—even in the church.

Even in the early church, monks were seen as a unique witness to the gospel's call to radical simplicity—but one not everyone had to follow in its entirety. But clearly monastic life offers the most holistic of environments where the extended family is a reality, love is practical, the poor and needy are cared for, and material addiction is curbed.

We are not all called to live such intense and cloistered monastic lives. But we are called to live in Acts-like communities with some expression of economic sharing and social holiness. Clearly the community in Acts lived in houses owned by private individuals who shared all things in common. They did not withdraw from the world or live life in a cloister but were part of their society. They dressed the same and went about their everyday life like everyone else, but with a difference. They showed extraordinary love for each other as well as all in need. The letter from Mathetes to Diognetus describes this well:

Christians are not distinguished from the rest of mankind by either country, speech or customs; the fact is, they nowhere settle in cities of their own; they use no peculiar language; they cultivate no eccentric mode of life . . . yet while they dwell in both Greek and non-Greek cities, as each one's lot was cast, and conform to the customs of the country in dress, food and mode of life in general, the whole tenor of their way of living stamps it as worthy of admiration and admittedly extraordinary. They reside in their respective countries, but as aliens. They take part in everything as citizens, and put up with everything as foreigners. Every foreign land is their home, and every home a foreign land.[2]

2. DISTRIBUTION OF WEALTH

In all the businesses I've started, I sought to practice distribution of wealth. Jubilee calls us to wealth creation (farming the land) as well as wealth distribution (sharing with the needy). Such distributions have been used for a variety of purposes, including buying houses, paying off mortgages, and securing pensions for missionaries. When I asked fellow directors in one of my Malaysian businesses to structure a share option scheme for our staff, they thought I meant the senior management. When I explained that I believe the cleaners should also be included, they balked, but to their credit, agreed. None of the staff—doctors, nurses, and cleaners—had ever owned shares in a publicly listed company before. They all had to be educated about the intricacies of share ownership, such as dividends, tax declarations, closed periods, and insider trading. One of our nurses sold her shares the following year to fund her son's university education in the USA—something she would not have been able to do on her

---

2. From a multichapter letter by Mathetes to Diognetus, circa 130 to 200 CE. David Otis Fuller, *Valiant For the Truth* (New York, NY: McGraw-Hill, 1961).

salary alone as a single mother. A salary alone isn't enough. Real empowerment comes through ownership of assets. That's what underlies the Jubilee program.

In recent years, many millionaires have been created through similar employee share ownership schemes in the tech sector (e.g., Microsoft, Apple, Google, Amazon). But an amazing example is the John Lewis Partnership, one of the most successful and largest retailers in the UK. The company's website states this:

> Over 100 years ago our Founder, John Spedan Lewis, began an experiment into a better way of doing business by including staff in decision making on how the business would be run.

> He set out the principles for how the Company should operate and produced a written Constitution to help Partners understand their rights and responsibilities as co-owners.

> Spedan Lewis wanted to create a way of doing business that was both commercial, allowing it to move quickly and stay ahead in a highly-competitive industry, and democratic, giving every Partner a voice in the business they co-own.[3]

All employees are partners and co-owners of the business to this day. John Spedan Lewis was revolutionary in the way he created wealth and shared it with all his employees. This is very much in accord with the spirit of Jubilee.

Julian Richer, the founder of the hi-fi chain Richer Sounds, recently sold 60 percent of his shares to an employee-owned trust and paid his employees bonuses of one thousand pounds for every year they had worked in his stores. The company also gives 15

---

3. John Lewis Partnership, "Our History," https://www.johnlewispartnership .co.uk/about/who-we-are/our-history.html.

percent of its profits to charity, which is remarkable generosity reflecting the spirit of Jubilee. Like Zacchaues's generosity (Luke 19), this would have amazed Jesus and made him smile.

But individuals I know have also, in their own small ways, sought to practice the spirit of Jubilee. One senior partner in a London law firm gave away his entire year's salary to a charity on his fiftieth birthday. That was him working out a personal Jubilee.

3. CANCELLATION OF DEBTS

The **Jubilee 2000 Movement** to cancel the debts of the poorest countries of the world resulted in US $130 billion being cancelled for thirty-six Heavily Indebted Poor Countries (HIPC) in 2005 by the G8 group together with the IMF. Since 2005, for the countries that had some of their debts canceled,

- Their debt payments have fallen from 10 percent of government revenue to 4 percent.

- The proportion of children completing primary school has increased from 51 percent to 66 percent.

- The number of women dying in childbirth has fallen from 680 per 100,000 births to 500.

This is clearly an impressive result. However, as was pointed out by the Jubilee Debt Campaign,

> Debt cancellation was vital in 2005 for countries to get out of the debt trap, and help provide essential services such as healthcare and education. However, nothing was done to prevent reckless lending re-creating debt crises, as is now seen in Europe. Governments continue to bailout lenders, incentivising them to continue acting recklessly, whilst giving large amounts of their "aid" money as loans.

Figures calculated by the Jubilee Debt Campaign, based on data from the World Bank,

> show that loans to impoverished country governments have increased by 40 percent in just one year, and have more than tripled since 2005.

> Lending to "low income countries" increased to $17.3 billion in 2013, the latest year with figures available, up from $12.2 billion in 2012 and $5.1 billion in 2005.

> Research by the Jubilee Debt Campaign, based on IMF and World Bank figures, has shown that debt payments for low income countries are set to increase from 4% of government revenue today to up-to 13% by the early 2020s.[4]

The debt spiral of HIPC nations is also true of individuals. Citizens of most developed countries, with a lifestyle characterized by overconsumption, are heavily in debt. Many debt spirals end in personal bankruptcies and broken lives.

Moral Hazard

What about the moral hazard of debt cancellation? This, of course, is one of the fears of the world's richest countries today. If they cancel the debts of the poorer countries, will they learn not to get into debt again? Will the rich nations find themselves worse off?

In fact, leading economists suggest that the opposite is true. Promoting the welfare of another, be it an individual or a nation,

---

4. Jubilee Debt Campaign, "Don't Turn the Clock Back: Analysing the Risks of the Lending Boom to Impoverished Countries," Oct. 10, 2014, https://jubileedebt .org.uk/report/dont-turn-clock-back-analysing-risks-lending-boom-impoverished -countries.

leads to an improvement in one's own welfare.[5] In fact, companies have their debts restructured all the time. Companies in distress often restructure their debts to avoid bankruptcy. Lenders have to forgive or cancel monies owed (called "taking a haircut") and allow more time for the loans to be repaid. Debt cancellation and restructuring are even applied to countries; recent examples include Argentina, Brazil, Greece, and Spain.

The biblical message on this point corroborates the economic facts. Wealth held onto does not bless the hoarder, it becomes a liability (Exod 16:20; Jas 5:2, 3). On the other hand, the wealthy will not go without if they share (Mal 3:10–12; Luke 6:38). Despite sharing what he had with a crowd of five thousand, the boy with five loaves and two fishes still had enough to eat himself (John 6:12, 13).

We can also practice cancellation of debts as individuals and churches.

Jubilee in Fremantle, Australia

A group of churches in Fremantle, Perth, Australia, felt God calling them to proclaim a Jubilee to the people of Fremantle. They raised over A\$80,000 and persuaded the utility companies to cancel the debts of those whose electricity, gas, and water have been cut off through arrears. On Easter day 2003, the utility companies wrote to their debtors and said that through the generosity of the churches of Fremantle, their debts have been canceled and their utilities reconnected. Because of the Data Protection Laws, the churches could not directly contact the utility customers. So, the

---

5.   For further study on this subject, an excellent resource is *The End of Poverty: How We Can Make It Happen In Our Lifetime* by Jeffrey Sachs (New York: Penguin, 2005).

utility companies included a letter from the churches explaining why they were proclaiming a Jubilee with a telephone contact for people who wanted to get in touch. The story hit the national television, with the mayor and church leaders being interviewed. The local radio station announced where families had had their utilities reconnected and the sums of debt canceled on the hour, every hour for the whole week—it was the most popular radio station that week. Many other acts of generosity were also practiced throughout the Jubilee Week. What an imaginative expression of Jubilee this was. This is the church living social holiness. This is the kind of church to belong to. It is relevant. It smells of God's justice and compassion for the poor.[6]

Jubilee in Singapore

Singapore's Golden Jubilee year to celebrate their fifty years of independence was in 2015. Care Corner, one of the largest social justice NGOs, together with the YMCA, decided they would carry out a debt cancellation program. They raised S$1 million, which was matched by the government, and canceled the debts of families they have been working with up to a maximum of S$2,000 and provided each family with a counselor for a year to help them manage their finances. Five hundred families were helped in this way by two hundred trained volunteer counselors.

The Methodist Church of Singapore also raised S$1.7 million to cancel the debts of 850 families for their 130th anniversary during the country's Jubilee year. A maximum of $2,000 was given to each of the families as a one-time gift to enable a fresh start. Gambling or credit card debts were excluded. The

6. www.ausprayernet.org.au/trans_articles4.php; www.fremantleJubilee.asn.au

gifts only covered debts related to daily necessities such as utilities and rent arrears.[7]

Both debt cancellation programs in Fremantle and Singapore are impressive expressions of Jubilee. But why do it only every fifty years? Jubilee is an everyday lifestyle in the New Testament. Perhaps a Jubilee every year, or at the very least match the Old Testament's requirement of every seven years. Perhaps even better, how can these churches incorporate even more frequent practices of generosity to create a community of social holiness?

4. SET THE CAPTIVES FREE

Sadly, there is more human slavery today than during the time of Wilberforce.

The International Labour Organization estimates that there are 40.3 million victims of human trafficking globally, of which 81 percent are trapped in forced labor, 25 percent are children, and 75 percent are women and girls. This is a terrible indictment of failure in our societies to protect the most vulnerable. The main reason remains that of poverty. So, unless and until we can address rural poverty, young boys and girls will be sold into sex trafficking, and many of the men and women who leave their villages with promises of employment abroad will be sold into labor trafficking.

Agape Connecting People (www.agape-cp.com)

Agape Connecting People operates a call and contact center inside the largest prison in Singapore. Its mission is to be a lead-

---

7. Theresa Tan, "Methodists in Singapore to Help the Poor Clear Their Debts," *Straits Times*, Dec. 7, 2014, https://www.straitstimes.com/singapore/methodists-in-singapore-to-help-the-poor-clear-their-debts.

ing provider of rehabilitation, reintegration, and resettlement services for prisoners, ex-offenders, delinquent youth, and socially displaced people.

Agape was founded by Anil David, who is himself an ex-offender. It currently employs 60 male and 120 female prisoners inside Changi Prison, Singapore's largest. Inmates who still have twelve to twenty-four months to serve are screened, trained, and employed in the call center. Rent is paid to the prison, and inmates are paid the minimum wage in Singapore of S$600 per month, which is disbursed when they leave prison. There is also a performance bonus scheme that incentivizes inmates. Once inmates are paid, many will start to send money back to their families, resulting in more visits to prison. The prison has initiated a six-month early release program for good behavior, provided that inmates are tagged and work in Agape's city call center.

Agape's city call center operates outside the prison. Suitable ex-inmates are re-employed when they are released from Changi. Because many of those employed in the city call center are ex-offenders, including members of the senior management, there is a strong sense of belonging. Ex-offenders don't have to hide their background and don't feel judged. They belong and feel accepted; this is their family. This sense of belonging, of being a family is critically important to providing the kind of support needed for these ex-inmates to not return to their old friends and habits. We see how the gospel's transformation of human community by solidarity in Christ leads to freedom. Through their connection to others, shalom can be brought to those with the deepest needs.

Agape is helping to rebuild broken lives, restoring self-esteem and confidence by equipping inmates with skills so that, on their release, they are better prepared to reintegrate into society and the marketplace, thereby reducing recidivism. Recidivism in the West ranges from 20 percent (Norway) to 65 percent (California) over a three-year period. As a three-year-old business, it is too early for Agape to be definitive about its recidivism rate, but current rates are running at below 5 percent. Agape speaks about forgiveness and the God of second, third, and fourth chances. Some are in prison because of bad decisions, others are there because of addiction, but there is grace for all.

Regenesys (www.regenesysbpo.com)

Regenesys in Cebu, Philippines, employs survivors of sex and labor trafficking in a Business Process Outsourcing (BPO) business. Survivors, 94 percent of whom are girls with an average age of twenty-three, are given computer training to do photo editing for US-based real estate companies. Data is downloaded from the US and sent back over night. Of those employed, 64 percent have children, and their salaries enable them to support their families. The business has two hundred employees.

Regenesys sets captives free from slavery, restores broken lives, invests in their training and employment, enabling them to financially support their families. God's image is being restored, they have dignity, independence, and are productive citizens of their country again. In addition to work conferring dignity, we discover that work also helps survivors find forgiveness.

Hagar International (www.hagarinternational.org)

Pierre Tami founded Hagar International in Cambodia more than thirty years ago to rescue women and children from trafficking and abuse. The stated mission of the Hagar project is "to foster hope for vulnerable women and children in crisis through holistic, transformational development and creative initiatives." Hagar was founded in response to the problems of street mothers and children in post-conflict Cambodia. It takes in women who have been abused and raped, rehabilitates them through a program of counseling, and then trains them to work in its growing number of businesses. To break the cycle of violence and poverty in Cambodia, Hagar uses an integrated three-pronged approach of rehabilitation, prevention, and reintegration.

Today, Hagar has more than six hundred children and women a year in its shelters. The Hagar Social Enterprise Group has started three businesses that today employ over three hundred people, mostly women. Employment helps these vulnerable women reintegrate into society, restoring their independence and dignity. One of Hagar's businesses is a joint venture with JOMA in Vietnam operating a chain of tourist-friendly cafes, currently employing two hundred people. Hagar's journey from social projects to fully commercial businesses with social returns has been both a painful and an instructive learning experience. Hagar now has a sheltered home in Kabul, Afghanistan, and will be looking to start appropriate businesses for the women there too.

Hagar's work is in three areas—rehabilitation, prevention, and reintegration:

- Rehabilitation: providing vulnerable women with the necessary life skills and income-earning capacity to transform their lives. They achieve this by providing a temporary home, counseling, training in literacy, numeracy, health, nutrition and vocational skills, schooling, and day care.

- Prevention: instituting interventions that avert women's descent into destitution, by providing training to increase employability, coaching in income-earning skills, children's and women's rights awareness, and job placement. All education promotes community health (including HIV), empowerment, human rights, antitrafficking, and anti–domestic violence agendas.

- Reintegration: mothers and their children are reestablished in mainstream society through livelihood opportunities in agriculture, self-employment, clothes making, or Hagar's microbusinesses.

Since 1994, Hagar has helped about one hundred thousand mothers, children, and family members through its social program and economic projects. Although funded by charitable organizations and governments, Hagar's aim is to be self-funding with profits from its commercialized ventures.

These three amazing projects, Agape, Regenesys, and Hagar, seek to work out the Jubilee instruction of releasing captives from slavery—sex, exploitative labor, or addiction. Survivors need a lot of emotional and psychological healing. But we see many broken lives and relationships being restored, human dignity and self-esteem recovered. This is Jubilee shalom.

In India, bonded labor and debt-bondage among the Dalits and Moolnivasis remain to this day. Generational debt among these lower caste communities has resulted in them working as bonded laborers in agriculture and brick making, but unable to pay off their debts. Are there not Christians who can find a sustainable solution to redeem these debts and set free these bonded laborers? Here is an urgent need for Jubilee action.

5. FEEDING THE WIDOWS AND FOOD DISTRIBUTION

As we have seen in part 1 of the book, hospitality for the masses and pilgrims at Pentecost was one of the unique features of the Acts community and later Christian care for the poor. Jewish pilgrims from across the Mediterranean world were hosted by local believers in Jerusalem. Then the apostles had to include the widows and orphans, and this huge undertaking got out of hand with complaints about favoritism and inefficiency. The apostles had to appoint deacons totally dedicated to managing the daily distribution of food. This was such a "wow" moment for the church. The church invisible had become visible. We often see structure as a negative thing, but the Acts community and later Christian poorhouses show how structure can be a means of Jubilee justice—a concrete embodiment of social holiness.

But why are so few churches practicing this kind of hospitality today? We attend church services and then retreat to our individual homes and eat our individual meals. Where is the going from house to house daily and sharing our meals? Where are the meals that are inclusive of the widows, orphans, foreigners, and singles? Shouldn't this be a distinctive of our church life? To do this, however, we will need the generosity that flows from our experience of the Holy Spirit. We will also need to think about how to structure our communities to embody social holiness and help others to hear the radical call of the gospel.

Immigrant Hospitality Programs

I was once an "alien" in the UK. I know what it was like to be an immigrant, and what the Bible teaches about welcoming immigrants is music to my ears. Unfortunately, many of our churches are not very welcoming or hospitable places. Friends International (www.friendsinternational.uk) is a great organization working with overseas students. My wife and a number of other women run one of their hospitality programs. Over the years, we have had thousands of overseas students in our house (and garden). What a richness these overseas students bring to our understanding of the world, and what an opportunity to demonstrate God's love and generosity. If we understand Jubilee, the church should be synonymous with hospitality, and Christians with generosity.

Mary's Meals (www.marysmeals.org.uk)

Mary's Meals is a wonderful charity that provides meals for school children in low-income countries. Magnus MacFarlane-Barrow started Mary's Meals in a garden shed in Edinburgh. He has now built an organization that feeds 1.5 million school children everyday in Africa, Asia, and South America. Their objectives as stated on their website are the following:

- Reduced hunger among children at school. Many children, teachers, and volunteers observed the positive physical effects that the school feeding program is making.

- Improved school attendance and the elimination of absences attributed to hunger. Our research found a marked reduction in the numbers of children leaving school early during the school day.

- Reduced levels of children dropping out of school. Teachers reported a reduction in the number of children dropping out of school due to hunger and observed that progression and completion rates had improved.

- Increased feelings of happiness at school and decreased levels of anxiety due to hunger. The percentage of children saying "I feel happy at school" increased from 60% to 81%, and 97% of children said having Mary's Meals' porridge at school had made a positive difference to their lives.

The church at Pentecost started a program of feeding widows. This became such an important part of the church's life that they had to elect deacons filled with the Spirit and faith to manage this huge program. Feeding the needy became a hallmark of the church from Pentecost, so much so that the Emperor Julian the Apostate complained about "these wretched Galileans—not only are they feeding their own poor, they are feeding ours as well." No wonder the church grew. The church was living out its faith by doing all the good they could. Mary's Meals is following in this wonderful tradition.

6. TREASURY FUNDS

Some churches still practice the common purse or treasury fund of the early church. This is a fund set aside for the poor to be disbursed by the leaders of the church to the needy. Many Mennonite churches continue to practice this. Every church should have a Jubilee Fund to meet the needs of its own members, but beyond that, to help those in an emergency. And it's not just money that is needed. The Citizens Advice Bureau (CAB) is a wonderful legal aid organization funded by the British government but staffed mainly by highly trained volunteers. It deals with all kinds of problems for ordinary citizens such as housing issues, debt, and quasilegal needs. During an emergency, cases may be referred to a group of local lawyers who have an emergency fund to tide people over until they can be properly assisted. Where is the church in this? Should not the church be *the* natural refuge for the needy? It was at various times throughout church history and in the Old Testament times. The poor were cared for by the structure that God had instituted, but humans dismantled and destroyed it by becoming like the other nations.

7. STEWARDSHIP OF THE LAND

Whatever our views are on the origins of climate change, it is clear we can't go on consuming and polluting at the rate we have been doing. Deforestation is occurring at an alarming rate, ocean levels are rising, fish stocks are a fraction of their former numbers, numerous species are now under threat due to habitat loss, overhunting and unsustainable agricultural practices are polluting our rivers, to name but a few of our current environmental concerns. And it is the poor who will suffer the most from the consequences of environmental degradation, despite having contributed the least to the problem.

The Jubilee provided for a year's rest for the land every seven years. The principle behind this regulation was so that we don't rape the environment and exploit our workers and animals.

Kuzuko (www.kuzukolodge.co.za; www.kuzuko.com)

The Kuzuko project combines conservation, job creation, and social transformation. It is located in the Blue Crane Route Municipality, where the main source of income is agriculture, the average income is half a dollar a day, unemployment is endemic, and HIV prevalence is 20 percent.

The Kuzuko Game Reserve is a 39,000-acre game park in one of the poorest areas of South Africa's Eastern Cape. It has a five-star lodge offering ecotourism and safari experience operated by the Legacy Hotel Group. It is a "Big Five" reserve in a malaria-free area and is incorporated into the Addo Elephant Park, the third-largest national park in South Africa. In addition to being one of the largest employers in a district with 70 percent unemployment, it employs a significant number of AIDS orphans, who are trained in a wide range of roles from game ranging to cookery and hospitality.

Farming in the arid climate of the Eastern Cape is a tough business. Kuzuko's land was once farmland, much of which had become seriously degraded through overgrazing. The land has been rehabilitated, and in partnership with the South African National Parks, game has been reintroduced with conservation programs for black rhinos, elephants, cheetahs, and Cape Mountain zebras. A program of reforestation with the indigenous spekboom shrub is also about to commence at Kuzuko. Spekboom captures carbon and improves water retention of the soil and has been approved for carbon trading.

There is a growing awareness among conservation agencies that, unless the economic needs of the poor around their reserves are addressed, their conservation efforts will not succeed. Kuzuko employs more than eighty people in secure meaningful work with the opportunity for progression. To date, Kuzuko has created more than 250 jobs through its conservation rehabilitation and spekboom reforestation work.

Kuzuko also runs the Kuzuko Foundation on its 1,500 acre Educational Park, which houses an educational center and nondangerous animals. With donations from guests and other sponsors, children are brought in for a day trip to learn about the fauna and flora and to walk with animals such as giraffes. The Kuzuko Foundation was created when it was realized that the vast majority of local children had never seen game in the wild. Because of habitat destruction, most game in Africa are now located in fenced reserves that are financially unaffordable for the poor to visit. It is hoped that through the Kuzuko Foundation, thousands of school children will be inspired and understand the importance of conservation.

AffordAble Abode (www.afford-able.com)

AffordAble Abode is a Malaysian/Singapore company that produces "green" building materials from the kenaf plant. Kenaf is a variety of the hibiscus plant that is very fast growing with a four-monthly growth-to-harvest cycle. The fibers are strong and are mainly used to make biocomposites for car interiors. Toyota and Ford both have kenaf biocomposites in their cars. The kenaf core is a waste byproduct of biocomposite production that is traditionally just burned as waste. AffordAble Abode have taken these cores, shredded them, and mixed them with lime to make a new material that is as strong as traditional cement blocks but 50 percent lighter. Using kenaf panels prefabricated in the factory, the company can build a low-cost house in four days. No cement or sand is required, avoiding the environmental damage of sand mining and the high greenhouse gas emissions of concrete. One can literally "grow your own eco house" with this plant. One hectare of kenaf produces enough core for two to three 100 square meter houses a year and sequesters sixty tons of CO_2 a year. For comparison, on average a car emits four to five tons CO_2 a year.

In addition to its positive environmental impact, AffordAble Abode is creating jobs for subsistence farmers and increasing their livelihood. This is good stewardship of the earth. It allows shalom to extend from human communities to all of creation.

Greenhope Indonesia (www.greenhope.co)

Greenhope is an Indonesian technology company that produces biodegradable plastic from cassava. Today's disposable society is built on plastic. While it is a fantastically useful material, the negative environmental impacts of our plastic addiction are now becoming painfully clear. It takes over two thousand years for plastic to break down. The plastic detritus in our oceans ensnares marine life, often fatally. Birds, fish, and animals often mistake plastic for food, strangling their stomachs with indigestible items. The plastic in our oceans slowly breaks down to microplastics, which then act as a sponge soaking up all the toxic chemicals and pollutants in the water. These microplastics are consumed by marine life, which we then in turn consume; on average we each now consume eleven thousand pieces of microplastic each per year. We have not stewarded the earth very well.

Greenhope's technology uses cassava as the source of starch to make a compostable plastic that biodegrades within two to three years. Their slogan is the 4Rs: "Reduce, Reuse, Recycle, and Return to the earth." Not only are they creating a more sustainable consumption and production system towards a greener earth, the company hopes to provide employment for two thousand cassava farmers and increase their income.

Bee Sweet Honey (www.beesweetltd.com)

Bee Sweet is an organic honey producer based in northern Zambia, started by John Enright. It supplies bee hives to small farmers and trains them to manage them. This outgrower program currently has around ninety thousand bee hives placed with ten thousand farmers. Honey is harvested twice a year and exported. In 2018 they produced 340 tons of certified forest honey for export.

The income is split between the company and the farmers. By achieving good export prices, Bee Sweet is able to provide farmers an additional income that is equivalent to as much as four times their total annual income from agriculture. This life-changing amount of additional income requires very little additional input from farmers allowing them to continue their other farming activities. The main investment farmers made with their additional income was on their children's education.

This business also has a positive environmental impact. Because of increased population pressures, deforestation for firewood is a major issue in northern Zambia. In order to produce honey, the bees need a healthy forest ecosystem in which to feed. Because of the income they receive from honey, farmers in the area have a greater appreciation of forest trees and are less likely to chop them down for firewood. The bee population has also increased as the number of hives has increased.

8. CREATION CARE AND CONSERVATION

Creation care is hardly taught in our churches today. We have misinterpreted Genesis 1:28 to "Be fertile and multiply; fill the earth and master it. Take charge of the fish of the sea, the birds in the sky, and everything crawling on the ground." We have come to equate "subdue" (or "master" or "have dominion") and "rule" as exploiting the earth. We picture an earthly authoritarian king ruling harshly, brutally (Ezek 34:4-5) and irresponsibly. But God's rule is that of a servant king. I believe a better understanding of the Genesis passage would be to "steward" the earth, because stewardship implies both responsibility and sustainability.

The Jubilee regulations to allow the land to rest every seven years have sound ecological rationale. With our intensive monoculture farming methods, relying on more and more chemical inputs of fertilizer and pesticides, we have damaged vast tracts of arable land, depleted the water table, and killed large numbers of insect pollinators. This is not the sustainable and responsible stewardship of the land envisaged in biblical creation theology. It is encouraging to see farmers turning to sustainable organic "zero tillage" farming, permaculture, and mixed farming in many parts of the world. Amazon Inc.'s acquisition of the organic food chain, WholeFoods, is a clear statement that consumers are looking for food produced responsibly.

On the issue of creation care and conservation, it is clear that conservation can't be tackled in silos, such as saving the rhinos or elephants or tigers. It needs to be more holistic and take into account the poverty of the surrounding community. Loss of species is linked to habitat loss, which is due to commercial exploitation and as well as poverty. Deforestation in many parts of Africa is certainly due to poverty. We have a saying, "If people are hungry, they will shoot your elephants and chop your trees." It's their rights. They were there before the conservationists. No matter how many rangers are equipped with AK47s, conservation will not succeed if people in the community are hungry. Furthermore, if conservation was carried out in silos without alleviating poverty, we reinforce the message that "animals are more important than humans." Jubilee calls us to steward the earth but also to care for the poor. Only then do we have true environmental justice.[8]

Gleaning Laws

The instruction at Sinai for the new nation to leave the edges of their fields for the poor, widows, orphans, and foreigners to harvest was practiced by Boaz in the story of Ruth, the foreigner. It would appear that this practice continued for centuries. In eighth-century England, this kind of gleaning was a legal right for the landless.[9] Today, Feedback Global is one of a handful of campaign groups organizing gleans across Britain. Due to the difficulty of predicting harvest sizes and timing, there is often a mismatch between the supply and demand of fresh produce. In the UK alone, it is estimated that 3.6 million tons of food goes to waste in fields every year—equivalent to 7.2 percent of food production worth £1.2 billion. Feedback Global is organizing teams of volunteers to harvest this surplus food from fields of

8. The lockdowns in many countries during the COVID-19 pandemic gave us a glimpse of what can happen to nature when it has a sabbath rest from humans. We saw penguins walking around Simons Town in South Africa, lions snoozing on roads with no traffic, mountain goats roaming English villages, dolphins in the Bosphorus, Istanbul, fish in Venice ports and canals without cruise ships, and so on. Perhaps there is wisdom underlying the sabbath year rest for the land.

9. Rebecca Wearn, "Could the Biblical Practice of Gleaning Cut Food Waste," *BBC News*, July 25, 2019, https://www.bbc.com/news/business-49098780.

supportive farmers. The harvest is then donated to food charities and food projects. Gleaning not only tackles food waste. It also provides a means of feeding those in need.

As I have tried to show, Jubilee justice appears in many forms in our time. Some live social holiness within their specific church community. Others live this in their work and activism. But these various initiatives show the transformative power of the gospel. Christ offers shalom to all, and it is the task of the church to create structures and practices to embody this social holiness.

CONCLUDING REMARKS

The Jubilee lifestyle as instructed by God through the covenant at Sinai was intended to build a new kingdom, a "holy nation," a humane and just society demonstrating how to love God and love the neighbor in practical ways, so that other nations can "see" what the true God is really like. But human selfishness was too demanding, and it was hardly practiced.

These outrageous instructions—one year's holiday, cancel debts, release slaves, and return all properties—are for me evidence of a divine initiative. No one wanting to invent a popular religion would make such demands and expect a mass following. No sane person at least. Imagine Moses going to the slaves in Egypt, stone tablets (Ten Commandments) tucked under his arms, proposing to lead them out of slavery, but they would have to live a Jubilee lifestyle as the new nation in relationship with God. I wonder how many would have followed him.

For forty days, at the top of Sinai, God gave Moses a series of instructions about how the new nation should live that God might dwell among them. Yet while this was going on, the people at the foot of the mountain were jeopardizing the new relationship with God by worshiping a gold calf (Exod 32–34). God's response was remarkable:

The LORD came down in the cloud and stood there with him, and proclaimed the name, "The LORD." The LORD passed in front of him and proclaimed:

> "The LORD! The LORD!
> a God who is compassionate and merciful,
>   very patient,
>   full of great loyalty and faithfulness,
>   showing great loyalty to a thousand generations,
>   forgiving every kind of sin and rebellion,
>   yet by no means clearing the guilty,
>   punishing for their parents' sins
>   their children and their grandchildren,
>   as well as the third and the fourth generation."
> (Exod 34:5-7)

The answer as to how God will be able to live among this sinful people is to be found in the Lord's name and character. The Lord is a God of love, mercy, faithfulness, and forgiveness. But this is not cheap grace. The Lord is also a God of justice. God's love and justice can't be separated, and the early Christians saw this most powerfully at the cross, where mercy and justice meet.

However, despite God's generosity while transforming this group of slaves into tribes and land owners, the Israelites failed to live as they had covenanted to live. The land was exploited and the poor were neglected. "Evil abounds," said the prophets. Inevitably, judgment came in the form of conquering empires, and the two nations were taken away into exile. The whole earth lost an opportunity to see what a truly holy nation would look like.

The exiled leaders in the fifth century BCE understood this forced migration as God's judgment for breaking the covenant. Some among the priests urged a return to the Torah instruction as they rebuilt a temple and fortified a wall. Four hundred years later, early Judaism emerged as the Pharisees developed commentaries with strict implications for Torah in daily life. Sabbath rest meant that you shouldn't walk more than a certain distance, you shouldn't cook or do any kind of work, including healing the sick. Some Pharisees during the time apparently even tithed the miniscule spices used in their cooking. Given their fervor for Torah after four centuries of Assyrian, Greek, and Roman military occupation, it was probably impossible to imagine a return to the one-year sabbath rest or debt cancellation or a return of occupied properties they owned.

The failed Jubilee program became a distant dream, a vision for the future when Messiah comes. And when the Christ came, he set out his mission in the Nazareth mandate and confirmed that he had come to usher in a Jubilee-style kingdom, where there was justice and mercy. How radical was his common-purse lifestyle with his disciples? As Kavin Rowe points out, Roman society had never envisioned such a radical solidarity between people of different economic and social status. This was the radical surprise of the gospel and unity in Christ.

But Jubilee was most radically seen when the Spirit came at Pentecost. God writes his teachings in human heart instead of tablets of stone to form a new "holy" nation. In effect, this was God's second attempt to form a Jubilee nation.

What do we need to do? Two things:

1. Eradicate dualistic theology from the church to understand that everything we have and do is sacred before God. As John Wesley rightly said, there is nothing secular except sin. We need a return to "body ministry" where our gifts in law, music, teaching, carpentry, plumbing, Uber driving, and business are recognized as spiritual gifts. God will require us to give an account for all these

gifts given to us. We can then collapse the hierarchy that exists in our churches with pastors and missionaries at the top and business and professionals at the bottom. Eradicating dualism will also help us understand that tithing our one-tenth is not enough. God is just as interested in how we steward our nine-tenths, because that also belongs to the Lord. It will help us see that holiness isn't just about praying and singing exuberant songs. Social holiness is about caring practically for the marginalized and the poor.

2. We need to be more visible as a community that cares for the poor and needy. The early church was the first port of call for them. "If you're hungry, find a Christian. If you are sick, homeless, lonely, find a Christian. They'll help you and feed you." For instance, I have a dream that all churches once a year will remove their pews and members bring food and clothes to create a storehouse so they can invite their neighbors, the widows, orphans, and immigrants to come and take what they need (Deut 14). Imagine what could happen if we practice Jubilee in this way. Imagine this as a national movement every year. Each denomination one day a year. And as we have over five hundred denominations, that's Jubilee everyday! And churches and individuals will surely have many other creative ways of living the social holiness of God's Jubilee.

So where does all this leave us? When the Spirit came at Pentecost, it brought Jubilee—creating community, a sense of belonging, of family. Cold, unwelcoming churches aren't communities, whatever they call themselves. Neither are churches that don't care for their poorer members and nonmembers. Jubilee challenges us to love our neighbors in a world of inequalities. And as we have seen, there are so many imaginative and simple ways of expressing

Jubilee—simple but costly, and only possible through the transforming power of the Spirit. Jubilee generosity and hospitality stand as a witness against our materialistic, consumerist society. Jubilee distribution of wealth will help to meet the needs of an unjust world. Jubilee community and belonging address the loneliness of our age. Jubilee shalom is a powerful antidote to a society propped up by anxiety medications.

If the Jubilee mandate was good enough for Jesus and the early church, we have both a corporate as well as individual responsibility to live out its principles in our church, work, and personal lives. The Jubilee instruction was part of the covenant made at Sinai at the formation of a new nation. Jesus and his disciples took this seriously and lived as a covenant community, working out Jubilee principles in the first century. We live in a different time, culture, and economy, but the examples in the second part of this book should inspire us to "go and do likewise" (Luke 10:37).

In the Old Testament Jubilee was prescribed every fifty years. But under the New Covenant, Jubilee is everyday. We are called every day to give rest. How will we be able to do this? Through a relationship with the One who is able to give us rest for our whole beings, through serving the needy, binding up the broken hearted, setting people free from all forms of slavery, and sharing our wealth. Jesus gives us the grace to live this radical, seemingly impossible call to social holiness.

May each of us be better stewards of our time, talent, and treasure, and better stewards of God's earth on which we live as resident aliens, and as immigrants.

BIBLIOGRAPHY

Chumash on Leviticus and Deuteronomy: Rashi's Commentary.
Jerusalem: Silbermann, 1934.

Craigie, Peter C. *The Book Of Deuteronomy.* NICOT. Grand
Rapids: William Eerdmans, 1976.

Ferguson, Everett, *Early Christians Speak.* Abilene, TX:
Biblical Research Press, 1981.

Griffiths, Brian, and Kim Tan. *Fighting Poverty through
Enterprise: The Case for Social Venture Capital.* Coventry,
UK: Transformational Business Network, 2007.

Jeremias, Joachim. *New Testament Theology.* London: SCM
Press, 1971.

Kreider, Alan. *Journey towards Holiness: A Way of Living for
God's Nation.* Scottdale, PA: Herald Press, 1987.

———. *Resident but Alien: How The Early Church Grew.*
Seattle: YWAM Publishing, 2009.

Murray, Stuart, *Beyond Tithing.* Eugene, OR: Wipf and Stock,
2011.

Rowe, C. Kavin. *Christianity's Surprise: A Sure and Certain
Hope.* Nashville: Abingdon Press, 2020.

Sloan, R. B., Jr. *The Favorable Year of the Lord: A Study of
Jubilary Theology in the Gospel of Luke.* Austin: Schola,
1977.

Stern, David H. *Jewish New Testament Commentary.* Clarksville, MD: Jewish New Testament Publications, 1992.

Tan, Kim. *The Jubilee Gospel.* Colorado Springs, CO: Authentic Media, 2008.

———. *Lost Heritage: The Story of Radical Christianity.* Ashford, UK: Anchor Recordings, 1996.

———. *Sting in the Tail: The Parables as Oriental Stories.* Ashford, UK: Anchor Recordings, 1998.

Tan, Kim, and Brian Griffiths. *Social Impact Investing: New Agenda in Fighting Poverty.* Ashford, UK: Anchor Recordings, 2016.

Wenham, G. J. *The Book Of Leviticus.* NICOT. Grand Rapids: William Eerdmans, 1979.

Williams, George H. *The Radical Reformation.* Philadelphia: Westminster Press, 1975.

Wright, Christopher. *Old Testament Ethics for the People of God.* Downers Grove, IL: InterVarsity Press, 2004.

Yoder, John Howard. *The Politics of Jesus.* 2nd ed. Grand Rapids: William B. Eerdmans Publishing Co., 1996.